Prophecy in Its Ancient Near Eastern Context

SOCIETY OF BIBLICAL LITERATURE

SBL

SYMPOSIUM SERIES

Christopher R. Matthews, Editor

Number 13

PROPHECY IN ITS ANCIENT NEAR EASTERN CONTEXT

MESOPOTAMIAN, BIBLICAL, AND ARABIAN PERSPECTIVES

edited by
Martti Nissinen

Martti Nissinen, editor

Prophecy in Its Ancient Near Eastern Context

Mesopotamian, Biblical, and Arabian Perspectives

Society of Biblical Literature
Atlanta

Prophecy in Its Ancient Near Eastern Context
Mesopotamian, Biblical, and Arabian Perspectives

edited by
Martti Nissinen

Library of Congress Cataloging-in-Publication Data

Prophecy in its ancient Near Eastern context : Mesopotamian, biblical, and Arabian perspectives / Martti Nissinen, editor.

p. cm. — (SBL symposium series ; no. 13)
Includes bibliographical references and indexes.
ISBN 0-88414-026-1 (pbk. : alk. paper)
1. Prophecy—Comparative studies—Congresses. 2. Middle East—Religion—Comparative studies—Congresses. I. Nissinen, Martti. II. Symposium series (Society of Biblical Literature) ; no. 13.
BL633.P75 2000
291.2′117—dc21 00-061927

08 07 06 05 04 03 02 01 00 5 4 3 2 1

Printed in the United States of America
on acid-free paper

Contents

Preface

It is common knowledge that the phenomenon called "prophecy"—transmission of allegedly divine messages by a human intermediary to a third party—is well attested, not only in the Hebrew Bible, but also in a number of ancient Near Eastern sources from different times and places. Up to the present, the subject has been difficult to study because of the virtual inaccessibility of many important sources. Today, however, the situation has changed. This is largely due to recent editions of the two major extrabiblical corpora of prophetic documents, the eighteenth-century B.C.E. letters from Mari by Jean-Marie Durand (1988) and the seventh-century B.C.E. Assyrian prophetic oracles by Simo Parpola (1997), which have made the sources available to all readers. Even biblical prophecy can now be examined, better than ever before, against its ancient Near Eastern background.

The seven contributions collected in this volume are published to provide all readers with recent information about the poorly known sources of ancient Near Eastern prophecy, and to open new vistas of research for specialists—cuneiformists as well as scholars in biblical and religious studies. The articles are based on papers read at sessions of the Prophecy in the Ancient Near East Group at the Society of Biblical Literature International Meeting in Lahti, Finland, on July 21, 1999. The two sessions were the first within the Society of Biblical Literature dedicated specifically to the study of ancient Near Eastern prophecy.

The temporal and geographical distribution of the sources examined in this book ranges from Mari of the eighteenth century B.C.E., to the Hebrew Bible, to Assyria of the seventh century B.C.E., and to Arabian documents from the seventh century C.E. The articles are written from manifold perspectives, including methodological, socioreligious, anthropological, as well as historical viewpoints.

The main concern of Part One is methodological; it concentrates on comparative studies and problems of definition. Hans M. Barstad considers the benefits and limitations, in principle, of the comparative method in the study of prophecy, and Lester L. Grabbe, using sources from ancient and modern times, illustrates prophecy as an anthropological phenomenon. David L. Petersen critiques current definitions of prophecy, emphasizing the transmissive nature of prophetic activity rather than the personal or societal qualities of the prophets.

Part Two discusses sources of prophecy from different periods. Herbert B. Huffmon surveys the parallel and conflicting aspects of prophecy and prophets in sources from Mari, Assyria, and the Hebrew Bible. Karel van der Toorn uses the prophetic sources from Mari and Assyria to demonstrate the theological differences between them. My own essay presents Neo-Assyrian sources that illuminate relations between the Assyrian prophets and the goddess Ištar, the king of Assyria, and the diviners. Jaakko Hämeen-Anttila deals with pre-Islamic and early Islamic attitudes to prophecy and the development of Arabian prophecy into the orthodox Islamic doctrine that regards Muḥammad as the sole prophet.

It is my pleasant duty to thank all the authors for their contributions, the interested audience of the Lahti sessions for proposing publication of the papers, as well as Greg Glover, Director of Publishing for SBL, and Rex D. Matthews and Christopher R. Matthews, editors of the SBL Symposium Series, for their kind cooperation. Special thanks are due to my friend Juhana Saukkonen for his able and accurate work in preparing the manuscript for publishing.

MARTTI NISSINEN
Helsinki, Finland

Abbreviations

A.	Tablet signature of texts from Mari
AAA	*Annals of Archaeology and Anthropology*
ABD	*Anchor Bible Dictionary*. Edited by D. N. Freedman. 6 vols. New York, 1992
ABL	*Assyrian and Babylonian Letters Belonging to the Kouyunjik Collections of the British Museum.* Edited by R. F. Harper. 14 vols. Chicago, 1892–1914
AcOr	*Acta orientalia*
AfOB	Archiv für Orientforschung: Beiheft
ANET	*Ancient Near Eastern Texts Relating to the Old Testament.* Edited by J. B. Pritchard. 3d ed. Princeton, 1969
AOAT	Alter Orient und Altes Testament
AoF	*Altorientalische Forschungen*
ARM	Archives royales de Mari
ATD	Das Alte Testament Deutsch
BCSMS	*Bulletin of the Canadian Society for Mesopotamian Studies*
Bib	*Biblica*
BSOAS	*Bulletin of the School of Oriental and African Studies*
BWL	W. G. Lambert, *Babylonian Wisdom Literature.* Oxford, 1960
BZ	*Biblische Zeitschrift*
CAD	*The Assyrian Dictionary of the Oriental Institute of the University of Chicago.* Chicago, 1956–
CBQ	*Catholic Biblical Quarterly*

CRRAI	Comptes Rendu, Rencontre Assyriologique Internationale
CT	*Cuneiform Texts from Babylonian Tablets in the British Museum*
DA	C Boissier, *Documents assyriens relatifs aux présages.* Paris: Bouillon, 1894–1899
DN	Divine name
ER	*The Encyclopedia of Religion.* Edited by M. Eliade. 16 vols. New York, 1987
FLP	Tablets in the collections of the Free Library of Pennsylvania
GAG	W. von Soden, *Grundriss der akkadischen Grammatik.* 2d ed. Rome, 1969
HBD	*HarperCollins Bible Dictionary.* Edited by P. J. Achtemeier et al. 2d ed. San Francisco, 1996
ICC	International Critical Commentary
IRT	Issues in Religion and Theology
JANESCU	*Journal of the Ancient Near Eastern Society of Columbia University*
JAOS	*Journal of the American Oriental Society*
JBL	*Journal of Biblical Literature*
JCS	*Journal of Cuneiform Studies*
JEOL	*Jaarbericht van het Vooraziatisch-Egyptisch Gezelschap (Genootschap) Ex oriente lux*
JNSL	*Journal of Northwest Semitic Languages*
JRAS	*Journal of the Royal Asiatic Society*
JSOT	*Journal for the Study of the Old Testament*
JSOTSup	Journal for the Study of the Old Testament: Supplement Series
KUB	*Keilschrifturkunden aus Boghazköi*

LAS	Simo Parpola, *Letters from Assyrian Scholars to the Kings Esarhaddon and Assurbanipal.* Vols. 1–2. Kevelaer, Germany: Butzon & Bercker; Neukirchen-Vluyn: Neukirchener, 1970–1983
LKA	E. Ebeling and F. Köcher, *Literarische Keilschrifttexte aus Assur.* Berlin, 1953
M.	Tablet signature of texts from Mari
MARI	*Mari: Annales de recherches interdisciplinaires*
MDP	Mémoires de la Délégation en Perse
MSL	*Materialien zum sumerischen Lexikon.* Edited by Benno Landsberger
NABU	*Nouvelles assyriologiques breves et utilitaires*
NBL	*Neues Bibel-Lexikon.* Edited by M. Görg and B. Lang. Zürich: Benziger, 1997
OAC	Orientis antiqui collectio
OBO	Orbis biblicus et orientalis
OECT	Oxford Editions of Cuneiform Texts
Or	*Orientalia* (NS)
OTL	Old Testament Library
PNA	*The Prosopography of the Neo-Assyrian Empire.* Edited by Karen Radner. Helsinki: Neo-Assyrian Text Corpus Project, 1998–
PTMS	Pittsburgh Theological Monograph Series
RA	*Revue d'assyriologie et d'archéologie orientale*
RB	*Revue biblique*
ReS	Jean-Marie Durand, "La religión en Siria durante la época de los reinos amoreos según la documentación de Mari." Pp. 127–533 in *Mitología y religión del antiguo oriente,* 2/1. Edited by P. Mander and J.-M. Durand. Estudios Orientales 8. Sabadell, Spain: AUSA, 1995
RHR	*Revue de l'histoire des religions*

RlA	*Reallexikon der Assyriologie.* Edited by G. A. Barton. New Haven, 1929
SAA	State Archives of Assyria
SAAS	State Archives of Assyria Studies
SBLSBS	Society of Biblical Literature Sources for Biblical Study
SBLSymS	Society of Biblical Literature Symposium Series
SBLWAW	Society of Biblical Literature Writings from the Ancient World
SHANE	Studies in the History of the Ancient Near East
Sm	Tablets in the collections of the British Museum
SSN	Studia semitica neerlandica
StudOr	Studia orientalia (monographs and article collections)
T.	Tablet signature of texts from Mari
TCL	Textes cunéiformes. Musée du Louvre
TCS	Texts from Cuneiform Sources
TDP	R. Labat, *Traité akkadien de diagnostics et procnostics médicaux.* Paris: Academie Internationale d'Histoire des Sciences, 1951
TSSI	John C. L. Gibson, *Textbook of Syrian Semitic Inscriptions.* Vols. 1–3. Oxford: Clarendon, 1971–1982
UF	*Ugarit-Forschungen*
VAB	Vorderasiatische Bibliothek
VS	Vorderasiatische Schriftdenkmäler
VT	*Vetus Testamentum*
VTSup	Vetus Testamentum Supplements
WO	*Die Welt des Orients*
YOS	Yale Oriental Series, Texts
ZTK	*Zeitschrift für Theologie und Kirche*

Part One

STUDIES IN METHOD

1

Comparare necesse est? Ancient Israelite and Ancient Near Eastern Prophecy in a Comparative Perspective

Hans M. Barstad

Background

Scholars have, during recent years, dated the Prophetical Books of the Hebrew Bible later and later. It has even been claimed that these texts are compositions from the Persian period and have little to do with a historical prophetic movement in preexilic Israel.[1] Moreover, increasing problems in relating ancient texts to any external historical reality, due to, among other things, the collapse of historicism in the humanities in general, have made it more difficult to make statements about prophecy as a historical phenomenon.[2] One result of these developments is that scholarly attention has focused increasingly on the extant corpus of "prophetic" texts from archaeological sites from all over the ancient Near East.[3] Many feel that these texts may also throw light on the study of biblical prophecy.

---

1 See H. M. Barstad, "No Prophets? Recent Developments in Biblical Prophetic Research and Ancient Near Eastern Prophecy," *JSOT* 57 (1993): 39–60. Reprinted in *The Prophets: A Sheffield Reader* (ed. P. R. Davies; Biblical Seminar 42; Sheffield: Sheffield Academic Press, 1996), 106–26.

2 For recent developments in views on history, see H. M. Barstad, "History and the Hebrew Bible," in *Can a "History of Israel" Be Written?* (ed. L. L. Grabbe; JSOTSup 245; European Seminar in Historical Methodology 1; Sheffield: Sheffield Academic Press, 1997), 37–64.

3 Among the texts most widely used for comparing biblical and ancient Near Eastern prophecy are those from ancient Mari, Neo-Assyrian texts, and a few West Semitic texts. The Mari prophetic texts are accessible in J.-M. Durand, *Archives épistolaires de Mari I/1* (ARM 26; Paris: Editions Recherche sur les Civilisations, 1988). The bibliography on Mari prophecy is enormous and cannot be provided here. For a complete bibliography on Mari, see J.-G. Heintz, *Bibliographie de Mari—Archéologie et Textes (1933–1988)* (Travaux du Groupe de Recherches et d'Etudes Sémitiques Anciennes [GRESA], Université des Sciences Humaines de Strasbourg 3; Wiesbaden: Harrassowitz, 1990). See also the following supplements by the same au-

The "popularity" of comparative studies has, as we know, varied over the years. Given the present situation in prophetic research, however, we must reckon it possible that we will see growing interest in comparative studies, at least in this particular field. For this reason, it seems worthwhile to reflect on some of the problems we may encounter in comparative studies of biblical prophetic texts.

This essay can hardly address the matter in detail; other restraints have to be considered. For instance, it is possible to characterize all human activity, in one way or another, as "comparative." There are, consequently, no limitations to what we may put into the somewhat imprecise category, "comparative studies." This statement also applies when we keep strictly to biblical and ancient Near Eastern "prophetic" texts. Even if we refrain from becoming too philosophical—which may easily happen—the word "comparative" brings to mind linguistic, literary, historico-religious, anthropological, and psychological associa-

---

thor: "Supplément I (1989–1990)," *Akkadica* 77 (1992): 1–37; "Supplément II (1991–1992)—Addenda & Corrigenda: Edition du 31 Déc. 1992," *Akkadica* 81 (1993): 1–22; with the collaboration of D. Bodi and L. Millot: "Bibliographie de Mari: Supplément III (1992–1993)," *Akkadica* 86 (1994): 1–23; "Supplément IV (1993–1994)—Addenda & Corrigenda: Edition du 31 Déc. 1994," *Akkadica* 91 (1995): 1–22. For the Neo-Assyrian prophetic texts, see the edition by S. Parpola, *Assyrian Prophecies* (SAA 9; Helsinki: Helsinki University Press, 1997), and the accompanying study by M. Nissinen, *References to Prophecy in Neo-Assyrian Sources* (SAAS 7; Helsinki: Neo-Assyrian Text Corpus Project, 1998). "Prophetic texts" from other ancient Near Eastern cultures are discussed in several scholarly contributions of varying quality. An excellent work (with bibliography) is M. Weippert, "Aspekte israelitischer Prophetie im Lichte verwandter Erscheinungen des Alten Orients," in *Ad bene et fideliter seminandum: Festgabe für Karlheinz Deller* (ed. G. Mauer and U. Magen; AOAT 220; Kevelaer, Germany: Butzon & Bercker; Neukirchen-Vluyn: Neukirchener, 1988), 287–319. See also B. Margalit, "Ninth-Century Israelite Prophecy in the Light of Contemporary NWSemitic Epigraphs," in *"Und Mose schrieb dieses Lied auf": Studien zum Alten Testament und zum Alten Orient, Festschrift für Oswald Loretz* (ed. M. Dietrich and I. Kottsieper; AOAT 250; Münster: Ugarit-Verlag, 1998), 515–32. Useful is *Oracles et prophéties dans l'antiquité: Actes du Colloque de Strasbourg, 15–17 juin 1995* (ed. J.-G. Heintz; Travaux du Centre de Recherche sur le Proche-Orient et la Grèce antiques 15; Paris: De Boccard, 1997). Still lacking is a synthesis of West Semitic prophecy similar to the excellent study by S. B. Parker, *Stories in Scripture and Inscriptions: Comparative Studies on Narratives in Northwest Semitic Inscriptions and the Hebrew Bible* (New York: Oxford University Press, 1997). Many observations in Parker's book, however, relate to prophecy. Related aspects are dealt with in A. Jeffers, *Magic and Divination in Ancient Palestine and Syria* (Studies in the History and Culture of the Ancient Near East 7; Leiden: Brill, 1996), and in M. Meyer and P. Mirecki, eds., *Ancient Magic and Ritual Power* (Religions in the Graeco-Roman World 129; Leiden: Brill, 1995).

tions. The literature in these fields is so vast and varied that it becomes nonsensical to refer to it in the present context. Instead, I ask a simple question: In what way(s) may reading "prophetic" texts from the ancient Near East be of value in our attempts to better understand biblical prophecy? Since my ambitions are fairly modest, I will not attempt an answer. I merely look at some of the problems connected with the question. In my view, the best starting point is to look at recent publications.

Taxonomy

A multitude of books and articles, in various languages, address comparative studies and the Hebrew Bible. Nevertheless, relatively few deal with problems of comparison in biblical research in a methodological and theoretical manner.[4]

When forced to do so we may divide comparative studies into two main groups. There is nothing original in this, and similar divisions have been made by other scholars.[5] Thus, we may classify comparative studies as "historical," for lack of a better word, or as "typological,"

4 A selection includes S. Talmon, "The 'Comparative Method' in Biblical Interpretation: Principles and Problems," in *Congress Volume, Göttingen, 1977* (VTSup 29; Leiden: Brill, 1978), 320–56; M. Malul, *The Comparative Method in Ancient Near Eastern and Biblical Legal Studies* (AOAT 227; Kevelaer, Germany: Butzon & Bercker; Neukirchen-Vluyn: Neukirchener, 1990), 1–78 and passim; T. Longman III, *Fictional Akkadian Autobiography: A Generic and Comparative Study* (Winona Lake, Ind.: Eisenbrauns, 1991), 22–36; S. L. Lieberman, "Are Biblical Parallels Euclidean?" *Maarav* 8 (1992): 81–94; K. van der Toorn, "Parallels in Biblical Research: Purposes of Comparison," in *The Bible and Its World* (division A of *Proceedings of the Eleventh Congress of Jewish Studies;* Jerusalem: World Union of Jewish Studies, 1994), 1–8; F. Bœspflug and F. Dunand, eds., *Le comparatisme en histoire des religions: Actes du Colloque internationale de Strasbourg, 18–20 septembre 1996* (Paris: Cerf, 1997). Mention should also be made of the several books resulting from seminars directed by W. W. Hallo: C. D. Evans, W. W. Hallo, and J. B. White, eds., *Scripture in Context: Essays on the Comparative Method* (PTMS 34; Pittsburgh: Pickwick, 1980); W. W. Hallo, J. C. Moyer, and L. G. Perdue, eds., *Scripture in Context II: More Essays on the Comparative Method* (Winona Lake, Ind.: Eisenbrauns, 1983); W. W. Hallo, B. W. Jones, and G. L. Mattingly, eds., *The Bible in the Light of Cuneiform Literature: Scripture in Context III* (Ancient Near Eastern Texts and Studies 8; Lewiston, N.Y.: Mellen, 1990); K. L. Younger, W. W. Hallo, and B. F. Batto, eds., *The Biblical Canon in Comparative Perspective: Scripture in Context IV* (Ancient Near Eastern Texts and Studies 11; Lewiston, N.Y.: Mellen, 1991).

5 There are many other ways in which one may distinguish among comparative approaches. See, for instance, the use of the terminology "limited" and "unlimited comparison" in J. G. Platvoet, *Comparing Religions, a Limitative Approach: An Analy-*

which also needs more specificity. When we make *historical* comparisons, we compare things within the "same" historic, linguistic, or literary context, within the same culture, social system, or civilization. Typically, comparisons between the Mari prophets and the prophets of the Hebrew Bible would fall in this category. We should, however, always keep in mind that a historical comparison must not (or should not?) be too interested in questions of origin or in whether a particular phenomenon results from cultural diffusionism. Such views, popular in biblical studies in earlier days, will, as a rule, be too speculative to be fruitful. Such views are based primarily on inadequate evolutionist ideas of how cultures grow. When such views are combined with value judgments about the supremacy of the biblical prophets, the results become very tenuous.[6]

By *typological* comparisons, I refer to comparisons between phenomena in different contexts, and from widely separated periods of time. Similarities among separate cultures would typically not follow historic-genetic connections, but rather would result from how the human brain works, and from how humans, for some reason, behave in "similar" manners in "similar" situations. I briefly mention one example. To make it easier for myself, given the necessary reservations, the example is not from prophecy. In the story about Jephthah's daughter in the book of Judges, chapter 11, Jephthah promises to sacrifice to the Lord the first person to greet him when he returns from having vanquished the Ammonites. Tragically, the first person to meet him is his only daughter. There are well-known parallels to this story in other cultures. The sacrifice of the hero's daughter reminds us of Iphigenia, the daughter of Agamemnon, who was sacrificed by her father to the goddess Artemis when the Greek fleet was deprived of wind off the Greek coast on its way to the Trojan War.[7] The sacrificial motif of *do ut des*, similarly, is so well-known that references should be unnecessary.[8] In the sacrificial logic of *do ut des,* extreme situations re-

sis of Akan, Para-Creole, and IFO-Sananda Rites and Prayers (Religion and Reason 24; The Hague: Mouton, 1982).

6 See L. Stachowiak, "Die Prophetie als religiöses Phänomen des Alten Orients," in *Dein Wort beachten: Alttestamentliche Aufsätze* (ed. J. Reindl; Leipzig: St. Benno, 1981), 58–75.

7 The motif in Jonah 1, in which Jonah is thrown into the sea and sacrificed in order to make the storm end, has similarities to the Agamemnon story.

8 See A. De Waal Malefijt, *Religion and Culture: An Introduction to Anthropology of Religion* (New York: Macmillan, 1968), 208–15. For an example from Rig-Veda, see

quire extreme measures. In the context of the ancient world, this includes human sacrifice. We know of a similar instance from ancient China, in which human sacrifice was required when a severe drought had lasted for seven years.[9] In the Jephthah story, then, we find several examples of what we call "typological" similarities. In view of the distinction just made, when scholars compare the Hebrew prophets and, for example, divinatory practices of modern, traditional societies,[10] these comparisons are termed "typological."

Comparisons between ancient Israelite and ancient Near Eastern prophetic texts have, for the most part, been of a "historical" kind. With the increasing interest in the social sciences in biblical studies, we will undoubtedly witness an increase in typological comparisons.[11] Some scholars of a more historical disposition believe that typological comparisons are less important, or less "true," and that little may be gained from them. Clearly this is not the case. Typological comparisons are simply different. There are, however, some problems involved. It may sometimes be very difficult, if not impossible, to decide whether a parallel phenomenon in two different but historically related cultures should be classified as "historical" or "typological." The categories in such cases may have to be combined. When we do find interesting similarities in closely related cultural systems, the similarities may result from how humans, as mentioned above, behave in similar manners in similar situations.

R. D. Baird, *Category Formation and the History of Religion* (2d ed.; History and Reason 1; Berlin: Mouton de Gruyter, 1991), 35–36.

9 S. Allen, "Drought, Human Sacrifice, and the Mandate of Heaven in a Lost Text from *Shang Shu*," *BSOAS* 47 (1984): 523–39.

10 Examples of, and references to, such comparisons appear in R. R. Wilson, *Prophecy and Society in Ancient Israel* (Philadelphia: Fortress Press, 1980); *Semeia* 21 (ed. R. C. Culley and T. W. Overholt; theme, "Anthropological Perspectives on Old Testament Prophecy") (1982); T. W. Overholt, *Channels of Prophecy: The Social Dynamics of Prophetic Activity* (Minneapolis: Fortress Press, 1989); L. L. Grabbe, *Priests, Prophets, Diviners, Sages: A Socio-historical Study of Religious Specialists in Ancient Israel* (Valley Forge, Pa.: Trinity Press International, 1995). For an emphasis on divination and power, see J. N. Bremmer, "Prophets, Seers, and Politics in Greece, Israel, and Early Modern Europe," *Numen* 40 (1993): 150–83.

11 As D. Fiensy has reminded us ("Using the Nuer Culture of Africa in Understanding the Old Testament: An Evaluation," *JSOT* 38 [1987]: 73): "Both Old Testament specialists and anthropologists have in some way or other compared the Old Testament with primitive cultures for at least 200 years." Fiensy is taking this information from the useful survey by J. W. Rogerson, *Anthropology and the Old Testament* (Growing Points in Theology; Oxford: Blackwell, 1978).

Method

When we turn to the more practical side, everyone would agree that sound method is vital for the success of comparative approaches. Yet I do not believe it possible to follow some scholars, who claim that we need a set of rules to guide comparative studies.[12] Each scholar needs to work out how to proceed. Method in comparative studies is no different from method in other fields of biblical study, for instance in exegesis; what is needed is craftsmanship and good judgment.

There are some principles on which we may all agree. Obviously, there should be a reason for making comparisons. We no longer need comparative studies of the "Frazer-Gaster type."[13] Many years ago, Ringgren wrote: "All too often, research in this area has turned into a kind of 'parallel hunting': the endeavor has been to find extra-biblical parallels for biblical ideas or customs—and as soon as such a parallel is found, all problems seem to be solved: the parallel is there, what more do we need?"[14] These are wise words, but are they easy to put into practice? Has there been a revolution in biblical studies since others before and after Ringgren issued similar appeals? I think not. It is, for instance, clear that many recent works do not move beyond the mention that similarities between texts exist, referring to the similarities briefly. Such short surveys of textual parallels may be useful when we regard them as exactly that: useful surveys. We should not, however, confuse such "lists" with comparative studies.[15]

Along the same lines, we find scholarly contributions that are far

---

[12] See, for instance, Talmon, "'Comparative Method,'" 356.

[13] The reference is to the aftermath of Sir James Frazer's *The Golden Bough: A Study in Magic and Religion* (12 vols.; London: Macmillan, 1890–1915). I am not considering that genre known as "Ancient Near Eastern Texts Relating to the Old Testament." Even if such tomes usually have more to do with the sales of publishing houses than with comparative studies, it is not necessary to disapprove of the genre, as J. M. Sasson does ("On Relating 'Religious Texts' to the Old Testament," *Maarav* 3 [1982]: 217–25). In my view, such collections are useful according to the quality of the individual works. A useful addition to this well-known literary genre is *Canonical Compositions from the Biblical World* (vol. 1 of *The Context of Scripture;* ed. W. W. Hallo and K. L. Younger; Leiden: Brill, 1997), scheduled to appear in two volumes.

[14] H. Ringgren, "The Impact of the Ancient Near East on Israelite Tradition," in *Tradition and Theology in the Old Testament* (ed. D. A. Knight; Philadelphia: Fortress Press, 1977), 31–46, at 32.

[15] Ringgren himself falls within this category when he gives scattered references to "prophecy" in Egypt, Ebla, Mari, Uruk, Assyria, Babylonia, Ugarit, Phoenicia,

more exhaustive, and that seem intended as comparative studies. W. Fauth, in a recent study,[16] gives a learned, useful, and thorough treatment of Hittite divination before he describes divination in the historical books of the Hebrew Bible, listing many interesting examples. There is, however, no real attempt to compare the Hittite and the biblical texts.[17] Fauth's work contains two entirely different studies on two quite distinct topics, both very useful, and both lacking a comparative perspective. Fauth's view on Israelite prophecy appears to be strongly influenced by the works of Georg Fohrer, which raises another problem in comparative studies.

When we compare biblical "prophecy" with "prophecy" in other texts or cultures it is always our own views of prophecy that we compare. The quality of these views may vary, to say the least. For instance, being an expert on biblical prophecy does not necessarily imply expertise on Mesopotamian matters. Even if we are experts, we have to consider that, as in most scholarly fields, there appears to be little consensus in prophetic studies. For example, two methodologically sound studies in the historical comparative category are those by Noort on Mari prophecy[18] and by Shupak on Egyptian prophecy.[19] Even though

Aram, Moab, and Deir ʿAlla, but fails to make more out of these references. See H. Ringgren, "Prophecy in the Ancient Near East," in *Israel's Prophetic Tradition: Essays in Honour of Peter R. Ackroyd* (ed. R. Coggins, A. Phillips, and M. Knibb; Cambridge: Cambridge University Press, 1982), 1–11. Another example would be the article by A. Lemaire, "Les groupes prophétiques dans l'Ancien Israël," in *Ancient Near East and India: Intercultural Religious Parallels (The Franco-Finnish Symposium, 10–11th Nov. 1990, The Finnish Institute, Paris)* (StudOr 70; Helsinki: Finnish Oriental Society, 1993), 39–55. Lemaire comments briefly on "prophecy" in Mari, Assyria, Phoenicia, Ammon, Moab, and Aram, and in the Old Testament, New Testament, and early Judaism, but does not compare the different groups.

16 W. Fauth, "Hethitische Beschwörungspriesterinnen—israelitische Propheten: Differente Phänotypen magischer Religiosität in Vorderasien," in Dietrich and Kottsieper, *"Und Mose schrieb dieses Lied auf,"* 289–318.

17 I was left with similar feelings after reading Wilson's *Prophecy and Society in Ancient Israel.* In the chapter "Prophecy in the Ancient Near East," Wilson surveys the phenomenon in Mesopotamia, Egypt, Palestine, and Syria in a fairly representative way, based on secondary sources. Since, however, no actual comparisons are made, I was a little astonished to read his conclusion: "The evidence that we have been able to glean from ancient Near Eastern sources indicates that intermediation in antiquity had some of the same features that are attested in modern societies" (133).

18 E. Noort, *Untersuchungen zum Gottesbescheid in Mari: Die "Mariprophetie" in der alttestamentlichen Forschung* (AOAT 202; Kevelaer, Germany: Butzon & Bercker; Neukirchen-Vluyn: Neukirchener, 1977).

19 N. Shupak, "Egyptian 'Prophecy' and Biblical Prophecy: Did the Phenome-

a student of biblical prophecy for many years, I cannot say that I always recognize the phenomenon of biblical prophecy as conceived (likewise differently) by Noort or Shupak. I am not saying that I am right and they are wrong—that is not my point. But we have a problem when scholar *A* and scholar *B* compare phenomenon *Y* to phenomenon *Z*, when they have widely different views on what *Y* is. One consequence is that, in any comparative study, one has to pay much more attention to what is being compared than has normally been the case.

I end this short survey by introducing another vital problem in comparative studies, exemplified by a model study by a distinguished "comparativist," Martti Nissinen, who has published several important studies on the subject.[20] Unfortunately, it is not possible to deal with his many interesting conclusions in detail.[21] I mention only one example. In his 1993 article on the relevance of Neo-Assyrian prophecy for Old Testament research, Nissinen identified many relevant similarities in the two corpora. In his conclusion, he notes that many examples in the Neo-Assyrian prophetic texts have few parallels in the Prophetic Books of the Hebrew Bible (with the exception of Isa 40–55).[22] The Historical Books and the book of Psalms, however, abound in interesting parallels. This conclusion is important not only for what it tells us about similarities between Neo-Assyrian prophetic texts and the Old Testament. It also has significant methodological implications. The method used by Nissinen is purely literary, based on "genre" identification. He restricts himself, in other words, to the in-

---

non of Prophecy, in the Biblical Sense, Exist in Ancient Egypt?" *JEOL* 31 (1989–1990): 5–40.

20 M. Nissinen, "Die Relevanz der neuassyrischen Prophetie für die alttestamentliche Forschung," in *Mesopotamica—Ugaritica—Biblica: Festschrift für Kurt Bergerhof* (ed. M. Dietrich and O. Loretz; AOAT 232; Kevelaer, Germany: Butzon & Bercker; Neukirchen-Vluyn: Neukirchener, 1993), 217–58. An important work by Nissinen on Neo-Assyrian prophecy, *References to Prophecy*, is cited in n. 3 above. See also by the same author: "Falsche Prophetie in neuassyrischer und deuteronomistischer Darstellung," in *Das Deuteronomium und seine Querbeziehungen* (ed. T. Veijola; Schriften der Finnischen Exegetischen Gesellschaft 62; Helsinki: Finnish Exegetical Society; Göttingen: Vandenhoeck & Ruprecht, 1996), 172–95.

21 See, for instance, Nissinen, *References to Prophecy*, 164: "In times of crisis the prophets encouraged the king with their words, proclaiming the love of the gods, particularly that of Ištar, for the divinely chosen king, and their support for his rightful undertakings, especially the military ones. But their words were not repeated only when the king's life or rule was in danger, they could be referred to in peaceful times as well, if a political decision required a divine authorization."

22 Nissinen, "Relevanz der neuassyrischen Prophetie," 249.

ternal reality of the text when making his comparisons. This is very important. Some scholars have unclear or unconscious views on the relationship between the texts they read and external prophecy as a social and historical phenomenon.[23] R. P. Carroll, in particular, has warned against this confusion, which appears most likely in sociological and anthropological models.[24] It is essential that all comparisons start from the literary level.[25] Only when this has been done is it possible to proceed and, eventually, to reconstruct prophecy as a historical phenomenon. Due to the nature of the sources and the highly stereotypical and conventional language of ancient Near Eastern literary genres, this attempt will often be more problematic than has hitherto been assumed.

---

23 A study like that of K. van der Toorn, "Old Babylonian Prophecy between the Oral and the Written," *JNSL* 24 (1998): 54–70, is, for all its excellence, sometimes problematic on this point. Even more problematic is the monograph by the same author: *Sin and Sanction in Israel and Mesopotamia: A Comparative Study* (SSN 22; Assen: Van Gorcum, 1985).

24 R. P. Carroll, "Prophecy and Society," in *The World of Ancient Israel: Sociological, Anthropological, and Political Perspectives (Essays by Members of the Society for Old Testament Study)* (ed. R. E. Clements; Cambridge: Cambridge University Press, 1989), 203–25. It does not follow from Carroll's article that one should not use sociological methods on biblical texts, even if there are also social anthropologists who refuse to engage in what they call "historical social anthropology." The important point is to bring methodological awareness into what one is doing.

25 For a useful discussion of problems relating to diachronic and synchronic questions in this connection, see E. Talstra, "From the 'Eclipse' to the 'Art' of Biblical Narrative: Reflections on Methods of Biblical Exegesis," in *Perspectives in the Study of the Old Testament and Early Judaism: A Symposium in Honour of Adam S. van der Woude* (ed. F. García Martínez and Ed Noort; VTSup 73; Leiden: Brill, 1998), 1–41.

2

Ancient Near Eastern Prophecy from an Anthropological Perspective

Lester L. Grabbe

With the first discoveries of prophetic material among the ancient Near Eastern texts, it was natural to compare them with the prophetic literature in the Hebrew Bible. This sort of comparison continues and will continue in the future, and rightly so. Yet one area that is potentially a rich source of comparative data on ancient Near Eastern prophecy has so far been neglected: social anthropology (often referred to in North America as cultural anthropology). The data from social anthropology have been applied to biblical prophecy, especially in recent years, but little attempt has been made to apply the social sciences to ancient Near Eastern prophecy.[1] I think this can be done with mutual benefit to both disciplines.[2]

My purpose is modest, since in a brief essay one can only give an outline. I discuss methodological considerations and then illustrate the potential value of anthropological data with several examples.

---

[1] For purposes of this essay, I concentrate on the Mari material, mainly as collected in Jean-Marie Durand, *Archives épistolaires de Mari I/1* (ARM 26; Paris: Editions Recherche sur les Civilisations, 1988). Further textual material appears in Maria deJong Ellis, "The Goddess Kititum Speaks to King Ibalpiel: Oracle Texts from Ishchali," *MARI* 5 (1987): 235–66. For the Neo-Assyrian prophecies, see Simo Parpola, *Assyrian Prophecies* (SAA 9; Helsinki: Helsinki University Press, 1997).

[2] For information on the anthropological study of prophecy, see my two studies, *Priests, Prophets, Diviners, Sages: A Socio-historical Study of Religious Specialists in Ancient Israel* (Valley Forge, Pa.: Trinity Press International, 1995), esp. 95–98 and 186–92; "The Social Setting of Early Jewish Apocalypticism," *Journal for the Study of the Pseudepigrapha* 4 (1989): 27–47. See also Robert R. Wilson, *Prophecy and Society in Ancient Israel* (Philadelphia: Fortress Press, 1980), 21–88, and Thomas W. Overholt, *Prophecy in Cross-Cultural Perspective: A Sourcebook for Biblical Researchers* (SBLSBS 17; Atlanta: Scholars Press, 1986). A number of individual studies are also cited in the footnotes below.

Methodological Considerations

It must be remembered—though it is too often forgotten—that the use of sociology and anthropology in our discipline has one purpose only: to provide a heuristic method.[3] Models derived from the social sciences are not data, but only a means of interrogating the textual and other sources. They allow us to ask questions in a new way and then to go back to the original sources, to see whether the questions can be answered. Such models are themselves the result of interpretation; they are not to be imposed on the familiar data but to be tested against it.

There are always dangers in such a comparative exercise, and, to help avoid them, it has often been pointed out that the first step is to compare systems rather than individual points of difference. Two details of separate cultures that seem remarkably similar may appear only fortuitously similar when each is studied as part of a whole system. Different cultures may map reality in a different way, so that episodic practices or beliefs become significant only when the total culture is taken into account. The comparison of isolated examples may give misleading results.

Yet we should be careful about being too rigid. Ways of viewing the world are sometimes strikingly the same in detail, even when the cultural systems are different. One example is the way the maternal uncle is regarded in a variety of cultures.[4] Without debating this particular argument, the observation illustrates that certain cultural elements may be similar, even when the systems are different, and that comparison of the isolated case is still justified. Nevertheless, the cultural system as a whole still needs to be considered, and the value of similarities at the level of details may be limited. The important point is to be open to a wide range of suggestions about the data, but to be rigorous in testing these queries.

One of the first difficulties in any cross-cultural comparison, in the

---

[3] I already have discussed methodological issues in *Priests, Prophets, Diviners, Sages* (14–19) and also in the article, "Sup-urbs or Only Hyp-urbs? Prophets and Populations " in *Every City Shall Be Forsaken: Urbanism and Prophecy in Ancient Israel and the Near East* (ed. L. L. Grabbe and R. Haak; JSOTSup; Sheffield: Sheffield Academic Press, forthcoming).

[4] Robert A. Oden, Jr., "Jacob as Father, Husband, and Nephew: Kinship Studies and the Patriarchal Narratives," *JBL* 102 (1983): 189–205.

case of prophecy, is the social and cultural setting of the prophecies and prophets to be compared. The ancient Near Eastern prophecies of Mari were delivered in a state headed by a king. The extant prophecies are often associated with the king or even directed at him, with court figures such as the queen, scribes, priests and other temple personnel involved. The king is warned to be careful; he is encouraged by being told that he will defeat his enemies; he is scolded for neglecting the deity who instigated the revelation. The prophetic revelation, which might be in the form of dreams or visions, frequently comes in the precincts of a temple.

By contrast, the prophecies and prophetic figures known to the social anthropologists usually have a different context. Many prophets have arisen during or in the aftermath of a colonial situation and can be grouped with "protest" or "millenarian" or "nativistic" movements. Even when prophecy was a native phenomenon, the data of how it functioned were often collected in the colonial or postcolonial situation, in which the native element had been modified or adapted. There was seldom a king, though there may have been a native leader of some sort, even if not officially recognized by the colonial administration.

A significant problem in comparing ancient Near Eastern prophets with modern prophetic figures studied by anthropologists is in having the actual words of the prophetic messages. Although the Mari texts often describe prophetic actions, both they and the other Near Eastern prophecies are characterized by using the words of the prophets themselves (see below on the question of *ipsissima verba*). Anthropological reports, on the other hand, often do not quote the messages of the prophetic figures verbatim. Instead, we usually read a summary of what the prophet said and did, often with occasions and settings lumped together to describe an ongoing pattern rather than the exact words said on a specific occasion.[5] This makes comparison of the messages in the two cultures more problematic.

---

5 Fortunately, there are a few exceptions. Perhaps the best is given by R. G. Willis ("Kaswa: Oral Tradition of a Fipa Prophet," *Africa* 40 [1970]: 248–56). Another source roughly contemporary with a prophetic figure and quoting some of his words appears in Jeremy Pemberton's work ("The History of Simon Kimbangu, Prophet, by the Writers Nfinangani and Nzungu, 1921: An Introduction and Annotated Translation," *Journal of Religion in Africa* 23 [1993]: 194–231) and in Donald MacKay and Daniel Ntoni-Nzinga ("Kimbangu's Interlocutor: Nyuvudi's *Nsamu*

Despite the difficulties, it is possible to make useful comparisons between prophecies from the ancient Near East and anthropological studies. What follows are comparisons in a variety of areas. As already noted, many prophecies from the ancient Near East in some way relate to the king. This is not surprising, given the context in which they were preserved. Prophecies about people of lower status or prophecies opposing the king were not likely to be preserved by state scribes or in official archives. The prophetic material that modern scholars discovered was in official archives and reflects the interests of those who assembled the archives or who ordered the material archived.

Selected Examples

Shamanism and Modes of Revelation

The various texts from Mesopotamia indicate a number of modes of revelation. Dreams of various sorts are a favorite means of receiving divine messages.[6] A good example is the Mari text reporting a dream in the temple of Dagan by a man named Malik-Dagan.[7] The message of the text, however, apart from the framework of the dream, does not differ from that of other Mari prophecies. Another example is the vision of the *āpilum* Qišti-Diritim, reported to Zimri-Lim through his wife Šibtu, although the broken text makes interpretation difficult.[8] Although today we might wish to distinguish between a dream and a vision, it is difficult to find clear differentiation in the ancient sources.

Receiving divine messages by dreams and visions is also known in case studies compiled by social anthropologists. One example concerns the American Indian figure known as the Delaware prophet (discussed in more detail below), who went on a journey and received a revelation. He insisted that it was an actual journey, but, from our perspective, some aspects look like visions. Another example is that of Handsome Lake, who founded a religious movement (called *Gai'wiio,*

Miangunza [The story of the prophets]," *Journal of Religion in Africa* 33 [1993]: 232–65).

[6] In the Mari texts, dreams are found in ARM 26 224–40. See also Jack M. Sasson, "Mari Dreams," *JAOS* 103 (1983): 283–93.

[7] ARM 26 233; Sasson, "Mari Dreams," 290–91.

[8] ARM 26 208. See Jack M. Sasson, "An Apocalyptic Vision from Mari? Speculations on ARM 10 9," *MARI* 1 (1982): 151–67; also William L. Moran, "New Evidence from Mari on the History of Prophecy," *Bib* 50 (1969): 15–56, esp. 50–52.

"good word") in about 1800 among the Seneca Indians of New York.[9] He became very ill and was thought to have died, but he awoke suddenly and told of a vision which included a visit to the afterlife. This vision became the basis for his new religion.

In some cases, the prophet seems to be the medium for a spirit's speech. This phenomenon has characteristics in common with figures known in other cultures as shamans and spirit mediums. Unfortunately, the term "shaman" is popularly used in a wide variety of contexts in which, during an earlier, less politically correct age, "medicine man" or even "witch doctor" would have been used. Although specialists do not agree on a single definition, the rather loose use of the term "shaman" in recent years is regrettable.[10] Nevertheless, many anthropologists would accept that the "central idea of shamanism is to establish means of contact with the supernatural world by the ecstatic experience of a professional and inspired intermediary, the shaman."[11]

The shaman was first recognized as a constituent of Siberian hunting tribes, and the word "shaman" itself was borrowed from the lan-

---

[9] General accounts appear in Brian R. Wilson (*Magic and Millennium: A Sociological Study of Religious Movements of Protest among Tribal and Third-World Peoples* [London: Heinemann, 1973], 387–97) and A. F. C. Wallace (*The Death and Rebirth of the Seneca* [New York: Random House, 1969]). Original reports of this vision appear in A. C. Parker (*The Code of Handsome Lake, the Seneca Prophet* [New York State Museum, Bulletin 163; Albany: New York State Museum, 1913]) and A. F. C. Wallace ("Halliday Jackson's Journal to the Seneca Indians, 1798–1800," *Pennsylvania History* 19 [1952]: 117–47, 325–49). Wallace has attempted to reconstruct the original vision from the various reports (*Death and Rebirth of the Seneca*, 242–48).

[10] Mircea Eliade has emphasized the technique of inducing a trance state (ecstasy) as the common feature of shamanism (*Shamanism: Archaic Techniques of Ecstasy* [Bollingen Series 76; Princeton: Princeton University Press, 1964]; Eliade et al., "Shamanism," *ER* 13:201–23). However, he has been criticized for focusing on the history-of-religions aspect of the problem without paying adequate attention to the sociological features of shamanism (see Åke Hultkrantz, "Ecological and Phenomenological Aspects of Shamanism," in *Shamanism in Siberia* [ed. V. Diószegi and M. Hoppál; Budapest: Akadémiai Kiadó, 1978], 27–58, esp. 30–31).

[11] Hultkrantz, "Ecological and Phenomenological Aspects of Shamanism," 30. Recent bibliography on shamanism includes Diószegi and Hoppál, *Shamanism in Siberia;* Carl-Martin Edsman, ed., *Studies in Shamanism* (Scripta Instituti Donneriani Aboensis 1; Stockholm: Almqvist and Wiksell, 1967); Juha Pentikäinen, ed., *Shamanism and Northern Ecology* (Religion and Society 36; Berlin and New York: Mouton de Gruyter, 1996); Caroline Humphrey with Urgunge Onon, *Shamans and Elders: Experience, Knowledge, and Power among the Daur Mongols* (Oxford Studies in Social and Cultural Anthropology; Oxford: Clarendon, 1996).

guage of one of these tribes, the Tungus. Although some would restrict the term to this specific context, to do so would ignore the anthropological recognition that similar social phenomena may occur in different societies. Shamanism occurs around the world but is restricted to particular societies.[12] It is found mainly in Siberia and inner Asia, North America, and South America. Although found sporadically elsewhere (Southeast Asia, Japan, Australia, Oceania), shamanism is not ubiquitous in premodern societies, nor should every prophetic figure or diviner in traditional societies be called a shaman. The main characteristic of the shaman is that he or she is a master of spirits. The shaman differs from a spirit medium in that the shaman actively employs the spirits rather than serving as a passive vehicle for the spirit. Nevertheless, both shamans and spirit mediums have a good deal in common, and some aspects of the Mesopotamian prophets find parallels in shamans and spirit mediums.

From the Mari and Neo-Assyrian texts it appears that some—perhaps most—of the prophets were spirit mediums rather than shamans in the classic sense. Both the *āpilum* and *muhhûm* appear in many cases to have received messages involuntarily. When prophets speak openly in a temple, this looks like spontaneous spirit possession: the spirit comes upon them, and they become a mouthpiece for the deity.[13] However, sometimes the prophetic figure simply delivers an official message,[14] while, on a few occasions, the king or official makes inquiry of the prophet.[15] In the last two cases, some prophets, especially those responding to questions, possibly were able to control the spirits to obtain a message. If so, they would compare well with the shamans of other cultures. We should be careful, since the texts are not clear: some prophetic figures may have taken the initiative to seek out and take charge of spirits. The immediate impression, though, is that the Mari prophets were mainly spirit mediums.

Prophets in a Monarchic Context

Few prophecies studied by social anthropologists relate to kings, because many were preserved in contexts relating to European coloniza-

---

12 Eliade et al., "Shamanism"; Hultkrantz, "Ecological and Phenomenological Aspects of Shamanism," 52–54.

13 A good example is ARM 26 213; cf. also nos. 195; 204; 214; 219; 237.

14 E.g., ARM 26 197; 208; 221; 221-bis.

15 E.g., ARM 26 199; 207; 212.

tion. In many cases, these prophecies appear in resistance to foreign domination, cultural influence, and imperialism. Nevertheless, a few relate to native kings and, more important, others have useful parallels to prophecies directed at ancient Near Eastern kings.

One example sharing characteristics with the ancient Near Eastern prophecies comes from the Kiganda religion of eastern Africa,[16] in which two levels of prophecy corresponded to "state" and "community," or to ruler and the common people. The prophets of the national shrines were mainly concerned with prophesying for the king and a few senior officials;[17] however, one figure managed to bridge the division between the people and the national shrines in the 1950s and 1960s.[18] Kigaanira began as a diviner but experienced a call from the god of war, who was usually associated with the national shrines. He prophesied restoration of the traditional king of Buganda, who had been exiled by the British colonial administration. The reason for the exile, according to Kigaanira, was that the people had turned from their traditional gods and religion. If they repented, the king would return, which happened a few months later.

Similar to Old Babylonian and Neo-Assyrian prophecies, which relate to victory of the king over his enemies, many modern prophecies are set during military action. Even in different cultures, prophetic figures have provided support for the political leader.[19] The data draw attention not only to what we know from Mari texts but also, significantly, to the areas where they provide little or no information.

One well-documented example is the Shawnee leader Tecumtha and his prophet brother Tenskwatawa, who clashed with the American expansion westward in the early nineteenth century.[20] The context is a bit different from that of the Mari prophets in that the prophetic movement began before military action, but it well illustrates what is missing from our knowledge of the Mari prophets. What helps is that

[16] Peter Rigby, "Prophets, Diviners, and Prophetism: The Recent History of Kiganda Religion," *Journal of Anthropological Research* 31 (1975): 116–48.

[17] Ibid., 131.

[18] Ibid., 133–39.

[19] Michael Adas provides a number of case studies from the Far East (*Prophets of Rebellion: Millenarian Protest Movements against the European Colonial Order* [Studies in Comparative World History; Chapel Hill: University of North Carolina Press; Cambridge: Cambridge University Press, 1979]).

[20] James Mooney, *The Ghost-Dance Religion and the Sioux Outbreak of 1890* (1896; repr., Lincoln: University of Nebraska Press, 1991), 670–91.

we have some more or less contemporary accounts of how Tenskwatawa became a prophet. In 1805, when tribes were being pushed west of the Ohio River and many Native Americans were succumbing to alcohol, a man who had been noteworthy mainly for stupidity and intoxication announced to friends and relatives that he had had a revelation. In the revelation, he had journeyed to the spirit world, at which he had been allowed to look but not to enter. The two young men who guided him gave him a message to take to his people, a message that included the renunciation of alcohol; the eschewing of white men's clothing, powder, and shot, and even the use of flint and steel to make a fire; and marriage between whites and Indians. He adopted the name of Tenskwatawa ("Open Door").

His fame and following spread over the ensuing years, with many tribes agreeing to return to the "old ways." His influence was important when his brother Tecumtha began to unite the tribes in an alliance against the continued encroachments of white settlers. Tecumtha started to organize resistance by visiting the various tribes, bringing the tomahawk which, if accepted, served as a symbol of support in war. The story of military preparations and political negotiations shows Tecumtha's astuteness and remarkable leadership, but this is beyond our purpose, except to note that he first attempted to negotiate with William Henry Harrison, governor of the Indiana Territory and later to become president, to have the Ohio River made the boundary between white settlement and Indian lands.

During one of Tecumtha's visits to the Creek Indians of Alabama, a chief accepted the tomahawk; however, Tecumtha judged that he was dissembling and stated:

> You do not believe the Great Spirit has sent me. You shall know. I leave Tuckhabatchee directly, and shall go straight to Detroit. When I arrive there, I will stamp on the ground with my foot and shake down every house in Tuckhabatchee.

After Tecumtha left, many natives were worried and convinced that something bad would happen. On the day fixed by Tecumtha's statement, there was a great rumbling. The people ran out of their houses, which were then shaken to the ground by the famous New Madrid earthquake.[21]

---

[21] Ibid., 687.

Tecumtha's preparations were short-circuited by his brother the prophet. While Tecumtha was away, Tenskwatawa declared war on the United States. When Governor Harrison decided to challenge him, the prophet performed rites that he argued would render Indian forces immune to the American bullets. On this basis, his warriors fought ferociously and bravely, but when they found that his assurances were untrue, they refused to listen to him and abandoned his leadership. His brother Tecumtha returned to find his hard-won following in disarray and his cause lost.

Divine Assistance in Military Endeavors

The promise of immunity from the weapons of the enemy, as predicted by Tenskwatawa, is known from many modern prophets who have supported rebel movements. For example, in the late nineteenth century, a prophet named Rembe was active among the Lugbara of Uganda. When the British took over in 1914, they received blame for outbreaks of various illnesses. Rembe dispensed a type of holy water that, ostensibly, would not only protect the people from the human and cattle diseases, but would also turn bullets into water. Unfortunately, Rembe was captured and executed by the colonial administration in 1920.[22] Promises of protection against enemy weapons are also known in other contexts,[23] such as Mari prophecy:

> Thus they (spoke): "A battle will not be fought. Right on arriving his (Išme-Dagan's) auxiliary troops will be scattered; furthermore, they will cut off the head of Išme-Dagan and put (it) under the foot of my lord. Thus (my lord will say): 'The army of Išme-Dagan is large, and if I a[rriv]e, will his auxiliary troops be scattered from him?' . . . Heaven forbid that my lord should s[ay] this, saying: 'By means of arms I (must) [lay] them [low].'"[24]

Prophetic Lifestyle

Another area in which social anthropology can be helpful is in prophets' behavior and mode of life. Such aspects as the prophetic call, the mode of revelation, and the prophet's continuing life and ac-

---

[22] Benjamin C. Ray, *African Religions: Symbol, Ritual, and Community* (Englewood Cliffs, N.J.: Prentice-Hall, 1976), 114–15.

[23] Adas, *Prophets of Rebellion*, 147–59.

[24] ARM 26 207:19–36, translation from Moran ("New Evidence form Mari," 48), reading *tillāni* in line 36. Durand translates somewhat differently because he reads *belāni* in line 36 (*Archives*, 436).

tivities have been documented in many different societies. Sadly, there are few data on such points among the Mari prophets, although, in one area, we have some information. Prophets are frequently noted for their strange actions or strange way of life. Sometimes this behavior affects them after they are called by the deity but before they recognize their calling; it is not unusual for such strange behavior to be the first signal that the deity has chosen that person. In most cases, we have no information in cuneiform texts on the call of the prophets, but the prophetic reports of Mari sometimes describe behavior or dress in ways that suggest differences from other people. One of the most interesting reports is a text describing a strange symbolic act,[25] in which a *muhhûm* of Dagan called for food and was given a lamb, which he ate raw. He assembled the city elders at the gate and described the devouring of the lamb as a sign of pestilence.

This is no more unusual than the Nuer prophet Ngundeng, who, during his prophetic call, spent weeks wandering the bush and eating nothing but tobacco, mud, grass, and dung.[26] At times, he also spent long periods sitting on a pointed stake. The idea that the prophet has strange dress or habits is well-known from the biblical prophets, including such figures as John the Baptist. That Isaiah wandered the streets of Jerusalem naked (Isa 20) was probably as strange to the city's inhabitants as eating raw lamb was to the city elders of Mari. There are many examples of strange behavior while the prophet is possessed by a spirit. For example, Verrier Elwin describes an Indian ceremony to drive a tiger away after it had killed a man.[27] At one point the spirit of the lord of the animals, in the form of a medium, comes upon the father of the dead man, and the medium begins to growl and run around like a tiger, at one point seizing a chicken, tearing off its head, and drinking the blood. In this case, the actions were performed by a temporary medium, whose actions did not represent his normal mode of life. On the other hand, the actions of the *muhhûm* described above may have been a one-time-only event; we do not know enough to characterize the situation.

---

[25] ARM 26 206.

[26] Douglas H. Johnson, *Nuer Prophets: A History of Prophecy from the Upper Nile in the Nineteenth and Twentieth Centuries* (Oxford Studies in Social and Cultural Anthropology; Oxford: Clarendon Press, 1994), 78–82.

[27] Verrier Elwin, *The Baiga* (London: John Murray, 1939), 300–304. Elwin's

Testing the Prophets

In a number of the prophetic reports from Mari, the person sending the report also sends a lock of the prophet's hair and a piece of cloth from the prophet's garment.[28] These items were to be tested by the normal process of extispicy to determine whether the prophet was genuine. This would have been typical, since it was customary to confirm any oracle by seeking another oracle or by seeing whether the same message was received through another form of divination.[29] Although testing the prophet was, consequently, part of the regular Mesopotamian inquiry into the future, it parallels the idea of not accepting the prophetic word at face value.

The Bible mentions a number of criteria for assessing the genuineness of a prophet or prophecy.[30] One of the most obvious is asking whether the predicted event came to pass (Deut 18:21–22).[31] I cannot call to mind an example from anthropological study in which a prophet is tested by divinatory methods, but it is clear that fulfillment is a major element in whether to believe or to continue believing in a prophetic figure. There are many examples in which the prophet's following disappeared when a major prediction failed to materialize; conversely, skeptics came to accept the prophet's authority when a predicted event took place (e.g., the prediction of Tecumtha noted above). Since many prophets have helped organize or support military action, defeat in an important battle is usually sufficient to discredit them, at least in the eyes of many followers (e.g., the failure of Tenskwatawa to protect his followers from the white soldiers' bullets).

Prophetic testing is often carried out in prophetic conflict. Although this might be slightly different from testing the validity of an

---

book has not been available to me, and the information here was gleaned from extracts in Overholt, *Prophecy in Cross-Cultural Perspective,* 253–57.

28 E.g., ARM 26 204; 213; 237. See also John F. Cragham, C.SS.R., "The *ARM X* 'Prophetic' Texts: Their Media, Style, and Structure," *JANESCU* 6 (1974): 39–57, esp. 53–55.

29 See, e.g., ARM 26 185-bis; 199; 207; 212, where confirmatory prophetic messages are mentioned or sought.

30 See Grabbe (*Priests, Prophets, Diviners, Sages,* 113–15) for a summary of these and also other criteria suggested by modern scholars. As noted, many of these are problematic—even contradictory—when considered further.

31 As will be obvious to many, this criterion is not very helpful since (*a*) many biblical prophecies have not come to pass and (*b*) prophetic fulfillment is often said to be contingent on the response of the people (Jonah; Ezek 33:1–20).

oracle, such prophetic contests are an important means of determining whether people still believe in the prophet. Jeremiah exposes Hananiah as a false prophet when Jeremiah's prophecy of his death comes true, while Hananiah's alleged prophecy that the people would return from exile within two years was shown false (Jer 28). The Nuer prophet Ngundeng set various tests, often of a physical nature, for those claiming to be prophets and coming to prove themselves against him.[32] Ngundeng had erected a huge earth mound about fifty feet high, with steep sides. He was apparently able to run up to the top of this mound without faltering, and one of his challenges to rival prophets was to do the same. Those who failed the test became his subservients, such as the female prophet Nyakong Bar, who was set to grinding corn and given as a consort to one of Ngundeng's followers when her power "disappeared into the mound" part of the way up.

Literary Prophecies

So far we have been dealing with "real" prophecies, those uttered by prophetic figures at a known time and place. But within cuneiform literature is a group of writings referred to as "prophecies," "apocalypses," or, most recently, "predictive texts."[33] Some of these writings (such as the Uruk and Dynastic prophecies) contain *ex eventu* prophecies and remind one of apocalyptic writings such as Dan 11. The problem, however, is not just one of "real" versus "literary" prophecies, because the distinction is not always clear-cut.

The difficulties are well illustrated by the recently published oracle texts from Ishchali.[34] There are only two, and much of one is broken off. The legible text (FLP 1674) is in the form of a letter from the goddess Kititum to Ibalpiel, king of Ešnunna, a contemporary of Hammurabi of Babylon and Zimri-Lim of Mari. It reads:[35]

> O King Ibalpiel! Thus the goddess Kititum: "The secrets of the gods are placed before me, (and) because you ever have the words of my name in your mouth, I continually open the secrets of the gods for you. At the advice of the gods, (and) by the command of Anu, the country is given you to rule. . . . Your econ-

---

32 Johnson, *Nuer Prophets*, 97–100.

33 See Maria deJong Ellis, "Observations on Mesopotamian Oracles and Prophetic Texts: Literary and Historiographic Considerations," *JCS* 41 (1989): 127–86, esp. 146–48.

34 DeJong Ellis, "Goddess Kititum."

35 Ibid., 240.

> omy will not diminish. Wherever in the land your hand has laid hold, the 'food of peace' will be secure. . . . (And) I, Kititum, will strengthen the foundations of your throne. I have established a protective spirit for you. Be ready to hear me!"

This format leaves many intriguing questions: Was the prophecy spontaneous or instigated? Who received it? Was it received as an audition, a dream, a vision, or in some other way? Yet it is very much like Near Eastern prophecies that begin, "Thus says (DN)." The message is that Kititum opens the secrets of the gods to Ibalpiel and will strengthen his throne and reward his rule with peace, increased domains, and prosperity. This is because the king has honored her by speaking her name. The content is thus similar to a number of the Mari prophecies. No demands are made on the king, however, except to continue to listen to the goddess, because that is what he has been doing. (One should compare similar messages from Yhwh to Israelite kings and others, such as Gen 26:2–5 and 2 Sam 7:8–16.)

The editor of the text from Ishchali has noted its literary character. Although deJong Ellis accepts that the text is probably based on a report of a revelation, she believes that the scribe has clothed it in his own literary form. Two points can be made: The first is that we do not know if this text was based on an actual oracle. The editor thinks that it was, but this is an educated guess. The second point is that even if the text were based on an actual oracle, the scribe may have provided the present form and wording.[36] This has implications for the question of whether we have the *ipsissima verba* of the prophets, whether in Mesopotamia or the OT. Even when a prophecy is based on actual speech from a human intermediary, can we be certain that we have the original words?

It is often difficult to distinguish between actual prophetic oracles and literary prophecies created by scribes. For example, even the Mari prophecies, which, in general, were written at roughly the same time

36 According to Durand, when the prophecies of the *āpilum* were written, they were couched in a more sophisticated language than would have been expected from the original utterances (*Archives,* 390–92). Simon B. Parker points out how those reporting the prophecy "did not always think it important to replicate the precise wording of oracles" and mixed interpretation with reporting ("Official Attitudes toward Prophecy at Mari and in Israel," *VT* 43 [1993]: 50–68, esp. 57–64).

they were uttered, were recorded by scribes who may have paraphrased or used stereotypical language.[37]

No one questions that texts like the Dynastic Prophecy are literary writings, probably scribal products, and are unlikely to have arisen in a temple or from a prophetic figure. Yet they are not that different from the prophecies recorded among the Mari texts nor from the recently published Neo-Assyrian prophecies. What they show is that a prophetic tradition has been adapted and used in a scribal text for a particular aim. This practice has an interesting parallel in what has been referred to as "prophecy" among the present-day Hopi Indians of the American Southwest.[38]

Knowledge of ancestral traditions (*novati*) is a source of power in the Hopi society. Leadership—both secular and religious—resides largely in possession of certain central ritual objects, but the one possessing them must also possess the associated tradition, songs, and ritual knowledge. One has to be a "sage" who possesses esoteric knowledge to hold authority in Hopi society. One element of tradition is the important ancestral myth, the "Emergence Myth," which describes how the Hopi and other peoples came from lower worlds into the present world. This myth is an important cultural artifact, used as a means of understanding the world and also as a basis for Hopi self-understanding.

Hopi prophecy is attested (probably for the past several centuries at least) and well documented for the late nineteenth and into the twentieth century:

> Hopi prophecy can be formally defined as statements about the future which were reportedly pronounced by the Hopi tutelary deity, Maasaw, and by the first people who appeared at Sipaapuni, the place of the emergence of mankind.[39]

Prophecies are given in several contexts: (1) in recitation of or reference to the emergence myth; (2) in ritual songs; and (3) in modern prose narrative such as pamphlets, newspaper interviews, and letters

---

[37] It is also widely believed that any genuine words of Isaiah of Jerusalem, Micah, Jeremiah, or other prophets have been edited, reworked, and supplemented by disciples and later scribes who passed down the tradition. The situation with ancient Near Eastern literary prophecies is not different from problems facing the OT scholar.

[38] Armin W. Geertz, *The Invention of Prophecy: Continuity and Meaning in Hopi Indian Religion* (Berkeley and Los Angeles: University of California Press, 1994).

[39] Ibid., 169–70.

(often as a form of rhetoric to influence European Americans). There are no prophets as such because there are no revelations in the normal sense, and certainly no ecstatic states. The prophecies are presented as predictions but are, in fact, interpretations of the core myth in the light of current events. Such events as the two world wars, the atomic bomb, space travel, and the like are alleged to have been forecast, though there is no evidence that such predictions were given in advance; rather, these are *ex eventu* prophecies.

Prophecy among the Hopi is thus hermeneutic of the myth. It encourages hearers to relate primordial times and conditions to contemporary times:

> The present apocalyptic conditions are identified with the primordial ones, thus fusing past with present. And this fusion not only confronts past conditions with present ones, but it also provides past solutions to present problems. . . . [P]rophecy incorporates contemporaneous affairs into the interpretive framework of prophetic discourse and subjects those affairs and the forces behind them to evaluation in terms of conceived tradition. This evaluation, or pronouncing of judgment, derives authority from tradition and serves as a mechanism in social and political strategy.[40]

Hopi prophecy is a means of interpreting society, its changes and crises, and also a means to change and shape society and its attitudes. The prophecies often have moral or spiritual messages, as well as social and political ones. Those adumbrating the prophecies could be said to function in many ways as "sages" and interpreters of sacred texts. Consequently, Hopi prophecy differs in many ways from the oracles given by prophetic figures; nevertheless, essential features are shared with the "literary prophecies."

Stereotypical Language

The language and messages of the Mari and Neo-Assyrian prophecies are remarkably monotonous. The same proverb ("under the straw, the water flows") is used several times in the Mari prophecies.[41] The king is told not to do anything without consulting the diviners. He is told not to fear because the god/goddess is with him, and that he

---

40 Ibid., 83, 165.

41 ARM 26 197; 199; 202. However, Parker argues that these uses are related, being three reports of essentially the same message ("Official Attitudes toward Prophecy," 57–60).

will overcome his enemies. This stereotypical language reuses a limited set of messages from traditional material. The language reminds one of the messages Native American resistance movements used to get Indians to return to older practices and to give up the "perverted" ways of the whites.

Smohalla, for example, arose as a prophet among an American Indian tribe of the Pacific Northwest in the mid–nineteenth century when there was conflict with white authorities over the native lands.[42] A concerted effort was being made to move the Indian tribes away from their ancestral homes and to induce them to become farmers and homesteaders. The religion founded by Smohalla may have been influenced by Christianity to some extent, but the fundamentals were those of the aboriginal religion in the area.

Although there is no evidence that Smohalla ever advocated violent resistance, he opposed the whites' plans as contrary to the divine will. According to him, Indian groups were given homelands by the creator, Nami Piap. A "holy covenant" existed between man and God. One of the conditions this placed on the Indians was not to divide the land, not to farm it, to sell it, or otherwise to disturb it after the customs of the whites.[43] He preached against his fellow countrymen who had abandoned the traditions of the ancestors and had become farmers. Like Jeremiah (6:16), Smohalla called them back to the "old paths," to obedience to God's laws as laid down from the beginning. He denounced law-breaking and violation of the divine covenant.

As already noted in the introduction to this article, the problem with finding good comparative examples of stereotypical language is that prophetic figures are seldom quoted explicitly in ethnographic and anthropological reports. There are exceptions to this situation, but they are few.[44]

---

42 Mooney, *Ghost-Dance Religion,* 708–31; C. E. Trafzer and M. A. Beach, "Smohalla, the Washani, and Religion as a Factor in Northwestern Indian History," *American Indian Quarterly* 9 (1985): 309–24; Click Relander, *Drummers and Dreamers* (with a foreword by Frederick Webb Hodge; 1953; repr., Seattle: Northwest Interpretive Association, 1986).

43 Mooney, *Ghost-Dance Religion,* 720–21; see also the extract of his description of native cosmology in Wayne Moquin (with Charles Van Doren), eds., *Great Documents in American Indian History* (New York: Praeger, 1973; reprinted with new foreword by Dee Brown, New York: Da Capo, 1995), 36–37.

44 See the sources in n. 5 above.

The Prophetic Call: An Example of Missing Data

Comparing Mari prophetic reports with those of North American Indian prophets is instructive, for it reveals what is missing from the Mari reports: information on the prophetic call or persona. The prophets in the Mari reports are ciphers without personality or background, even if we often know their names and even professions. Yet if the analogy with prophets in other cultures has validity, the Mari prophets must in most cases have encountered the divine prior to their written revelations. This may not apply to the *šangû*-priest who received a revelation while sleeping in the temple, but, for most of the *muhhûm*, the type of call known among shamans and spirit mediums everywhere probably lies behind revelations reported in the Mari letters.

The importance of this experience can be gleaned from the reports about the call of another Amerindian figure, the Delaware prophet. His message was similar to Tenskwatawa's; indeed, because he prophesied not long before Tenskwatawa, one could argue for a strong influence on the latter. In any case, the information on the Delaware prophet's call has reached us in much more detail. He was sought for seeking to know the "Master of Life" and for a journey westward in hopes of finding him. After journeying for many days, he claims to have been guided to the Master of Life on the top of a mountain (he always argued that this was not a vision, but an actual experience), where he was told to tell his people to give up polygamy, drunkenness, white men's clothing, the use of flint and steel to make fire, and fighting among themselves. He preached the following message, which he claimed to have received in person from the Master of Life:

> Hear what the Great Spirit has ordered me to tell you! You are to make sacrifices, in the manner that I shall direct; to put off entirely from yourselves the customs which you have adopted since the white people came among us. You are to return to that former happy state, in which we lived in peace and plenty, before these strangers came to disturb us; and, above all, you must abstain from drinking their deadly *beson*, which they have forced upon us, for the sake of increasing their gains and diminishing our numbers. Then will the Great Spirit give success to our arms; then he will give us strength to conquer our enemies, to drive them from hence, and recover the passage to the heavenly regions which they have taken from us.[45]

The Delaware prophet apparently also had seen a picture of paradise

---

[45] Mooney, *Ghost-Dance Religion*, 667.

and hell, which he depicted on a small buckskin map that he would draw and sell to his hearers.

One cannot help wondering what spiritual journey and encounter with the divine the Mari prophets might have described if they had had the opportunity. We must assume that most, at some point, experienced what can be described as a "call." It is unlikely that their messages were one-time events, without an encounter with the divine in the background or context in which the message was received. All of this data is part of the "call" experience and changes the individual's life forever. This aspect of the prophetic tradition is a question begged by the Mari data, but we need to keep our eyes open for hints.[46]

Reactions to Failure of Prophecy: Another Example of Missing Data

Among the prophecies from Mari are several addressed to the Mari king Zimri-Lim, which predict that he will defeat his enemies Babylon and its king, Hammurabi. One says:

> . . . and then the *aplûm* of Dagan of Tut[tul] arose and spoke as follows: "O Babylon! How must you be constantly treated? I am going to gather you into a net. . . . I will d[eli]ver into the power of Zimri-Li[m] the houses of the seven confederates and all their poss<ess>ions."[47]

This was a false prophecy, as we know: Hammurabi and the Babylonians defeated Zimri-Lim and took control of Mari. Zimri-Lim's palace, and probably much of the city, was burned. We read no further of Zimri-Lim and do not know what happened to him.

This absence makes us realize that another piece of information is missing from present data on Mari: the explanation of why the prophecies failed. This is illustrated by considering the aftermath of the Spanish conquest of King Montezuma and the Aztecs of Mexico.[48] Our knowledge of an apparent prophetic tradition among the Aztecs,

---

[46] In the discussion when this paper was presented in Lahti, Herbert Huffmon suggested that the nature of the texts precluded this sort of information from having been recorded. I agree that the nature of the texts is the main problem, but I would argue that we should be alert in case something slipped through, which we might overlook if we were not aware of the question.

[47] ARM 26 209; quote from *ANET*, 625.

[48] For my information, I am dependent on Stephen A. Colston, "'No Longer Will There Be a Mexico': Omens, Prophecies, and the Conquest of the Aztec Empire," *American Indian Quarterly* 9 (1985): 239–58.

unfortunately, is all from postcolonial sources. This makes determining the original prophecies problematic, although some aspects can be determined with reasonable certainty. A copy of a preconquest history, called the Florentine Codex, mentions eight omens that preceded the arrival of Cortez. The conquest was not just a case of superior foreigners overcoming unsophisticated and backward natives; rather, there had been warnings of disaster. This disaster was brought on because the god Huitzilopochtli had abandoned his people, a fate facilitated by the arrogance of the last ruler, Montezuma.

After the fall of Mari, there likely were those who wondered about Mari's own prophecies, and perhaps some of the prophetic figures themselves were perplexed about their own revelations. The chances are that some sort of post-trauma analysis took place among the survivors. This postmortem and perhaps a necessary reinterpretation of prophecy are presently missing from the Mari texts.[49]

Conclusions

I have tried to illustrate the potential value of social anthropology in better understanding ancient Near Eastern prophecy. Some of the examples may be more convincing than others, but the point is that they show how cross-cultural comparisons can sometimes be helpful. Such comparison will not add to the data, for any theory or interpretation must be based on the ancient texts themselves. Comparative examples from the social sciences suggest new ways of interrogating the data and a broader context for examining the phenomena extracted from the specific texts.

As the examples above indicate, comparison can be made on a variety of levels. The most helpful level is comparison of entire cultures. This may not be practical, however, especially when cultures differ significantly or when little is known of one or both. More practical in most cases is the comparison of similar phenomena in two or more cultures, such as divinatory practices or prophetism.

---

49 Robert P. Carroll discusses the various ways in which prophets and writers may have dealt with the "failure" of prophecy (*When Prophecy Failed* [London: SPCK, 1979]). He applies theories developed by Leon Festinger in *A Theory of Cognitive Dissonance* (London: Tavistock, 1962) and by Leon Festinger, Henry W. Riecken, and Stanley Schachter in *When Prophecy Fails: A Social and Psychological Study of a Modern Group That Predicted the Destruction of the World* (Minneapolis: University of Minnesota Press, 1956).

Finally, specific cultural artifacts (detailed practices, views, rites) can be compared. These are the most hazardous comparisons in the sense that similarities or differences may be superficial and have no significance when the entire society is taken into account. Nevertheless, study has found some shared details in societies which are otherwise rather diverse in structure. For example, it is common for prophetic figures to exhibit behavior that would normally be considered odd or even unacceptable. This seems, across many different societies, to be a part of the prophetic persona. More important from our point of view, almost all such figures experience some sort of call. We do not have this information for the Mari prophets, but it might be useful to search for.

Cross-cultural comparisons can sometimes be made because one culture has influenced the other. Although it is theoretically possible that Mari and/or the Neo-Assyrian prophecies influenced Israel, the distance in time and space makes this unlikely. Similar conditions and situations, however, may yield similar results without cultural contact; direct or indirect influence does not have to be assumed. Anthropological comparison with ancient Near Eastern prophecy has only begun. The recent publication of textual material makes the contributions of the social sciences more important in getting the most out of these new data.

3

Defining Prophecy and Prophetic Literature

David L. Petersen

As the new millennium begins, it seems appropriate to determine gains in our understanding of prophecy and prophetic literature, particularly as we seek to comprehend these phenomena in Israel and in the larger ancient Near Eastern environment. In this essay, I do several things. First, I offer a typology of different ways in which prophets have been defined or understood. During this discussion, I advocate the notion of prophet as intermediary. Second, I review one recent definition, which appears in the *Neues Bibel-Lexikon* article on prophecy in the ancient Near East, to examine its place in this typology. Third, I offer a few basic comments about biblical prophetic literature that grow out of an assessment of prophets as intermediaries. Fourth, and finally, I make several observations about the relationship between prophecy and prophetic literature in ancient Mesopotamia and that in ancient Israel.

Typology

Biblical scholars, both present and past, have created different definitions of what it means to be a prophet. At the outset, I offer a sixfold typology of definitions that might help set the stage for a new period of studies in prophecy and prophetic literature.

1. The prophet has an intense experience of the deity. This notion has worked itself out in various ways. Influential early proponents of this view were Hermann Gunkel and Gustav Hölscher. Gunkel published several versions of his ideas, the first appearing in 1903.[1] He maintained that the prophets had distinctive, usually private, experiences in which the deity was revealed to them. These experiences were, in

[1] H. Gunkel, "Die geheimen Erfahrungen der Propheten Israels: Eine religionspsychologische Studie," *Das Suchen der Zeit: Blätter Deutscher Zukunft* 1 (1903): 112–53.

theory, hidden from others, but they could involve external manifestations. Gunkel used the term "ecstasy" to describe this experience, a term that to this day has remained prominent in discussions of prophets. In similar fashion, Hölscher, influenced by the writings of Wilhelm Wundt, maintained that the key to understanding Israel's prophets was to place them within a psychological category, which he too named "ecstasy."[2]

Probably the most influential version of this approach, which views prophecy as an especially intense form of religious behavior, has been that of Johannes Lindblom. As did Hölscher, Lindblom noted affinities between the experiences of Israel's prophets and individuals who have "supernormal experiences." Lindblom defines a prophet as "a person who, because he is conscious of having been specially chosen and called, feels forced to perform actions and proclaim ideas which, in a mental state of intense inspiration or real ecstasy, have been indicated to him in the form of divine relations."[3]

Influential though this view has been, serious questions have been raised. Is ecstasy or state of possession a common denominator or *sine qua non* for all prophetic behavior? It seems clear that much of what prophets did involved behavior apart from ecstasy, for example, Isaiah walking and talking with the king (Isa 7). Further, much prophetic literature offers no direct evidence of extraordinary emotional involvement. In sum, though some prophetic behavior might be characterized as ecstasy (or a state of possession), ecstasy is not a hallmark of all prophetic activity.

2. *The prophet speaks or writes in a distinctive way.* Here the focus has been on the literature attributed to prophets, much of it poetic. Attention to Hebrew Bible poetic literature has, perforce, had an impact on notions of prophecy; one should note especially the work of Johann Gottfried Herder.[4] However, there have been more recent proponents of this view. Some scholars refer to a poetic spirit as the source of prophetic activity. Abraham Heschel provided a classic exposition of this position, writing that "the prophet is a poet" or "prophecy is po-

---

2 G. Hölscher, *Die Propheten: Untersuchungen zur religionsgeschichte Israels* (Leipzig: J. Hinrichs, 1914).

3 J. Lindblom, *Prophecy in Ancient Israel* (Philadelphia: Fortress Press, 1962), 46.

4 J. G. Herder, *The Spirit of Hebrew Poetry* (2 vols.; 1782–1783; Burlington, Va.: E. Smith, 1833).

etry."[5] More recently, David Noel Freedman wrote that "poetry and prophecy in the biblical tradition share so many of the same features and overlap to such an extent that one cannot be understood in terms of the other. Poetry was the central medium of prophecy."[6]

To be sure, considerable prophetic literature is written in poetry. However, many forms of prophetic literature occur in prose: the vision report and the prophetic legend, to name two prominent examples. As Yehoshua Gitay has demonstrated, the self-conscious use of prose in a prophetic text, for example, in Isa 8, serves the prophet's rhetorical interests.[7] To argue that prophetic literature may be equated with poetry is to ignore constitutive elements of prophetic behavior and literature. Hence, we should take care to avoid thinking that prophets were essentially poets. They could act in a manner that resulted in the creation of prose as well as poetry.

3. The prophet acts in a particular social setting. This notion grew initially out of form-critical observations and may be traced to the vigorous logic of Sigmund Mowinckel.[8] Mowinckel followed up on a claim of Gunkel, namely, that there were prophetic elements in the Psalms. What Gunkel deemed to be a literary relationship—a psalmist borrowing language from prophetic books—was for Mowinckel a social reality. Mowinckel contended that prophets were cultic officials, priests active at the temple. Put another way, prophets, according to Mowinckel, were active in a particular social setting. Mowinckel's theory sparked what has come to be known as the "cultic prophecy thesis."

There have, however, been other claims for a prophetic social setting. For example, Frank Cross argued that prophets were embedded in the royal institutions of ancient Israel.[9] They were involved early on in military activity, in designating kings, and in making judgments on

---

[5] A. Heschel, *The Prophets* (New York: Harper & Row, 1962).

[6] D. Freedman offers these judgments in "Pottery, Poetry, and Prophecy: An Essay on Biblical Poetry," *JBL* 96 (1977): 5–26, and in "Discourse on Prophetic Discourse," in *The Quest for the Kingdom of God: Studies in Honor of George E. Mendenhall* (ed. H. Huffmon et al.; Winona Lake, Ind.: Eisenbrauns, 1983), 141–58.

[7] Y. Gitay, "Oratorical Rhetoric: The Question of Prophetic Language with Special Attention to Isaiah," *Amsterdamse Cahiers* 10 (1989): 72–83.

[8] S. Mowinckel, *Psalmenstudien III: Kultprophtie und prophetische Psalmen* (Kristiania, Norway: Jacob Dybwad, 1923).

[9] F. Cross, *Canaanite Myth and Hebrew Epic* (Cambridge: Harvard University Press, 1973), 223–29.

royal individuals. Though these functions changed over time, prophets remained close to this center of Israelite society. Cross thought it significant that prophecy commenced in Israel at about the same time as monarchy, and that it ceased at about the same time that the monarchy disappeared.

Both Mowinckel and Cross maintained that the prophets were inextricably linked to specific social contexts, the cult and the monarchy, respectively. Here too one must raise questions. To be sure, some prophets were priests, most clearly Jeremiah, Ezekiel, and Zechariah. The book of Joel surely reflects ritual activity that took place at the temple. However, what was true for some prophets in this vein was not true for all.

There is one important corollary to theses of the sort adumbrated by Mowinckel and Cross. If prophets are active in a particular social setting and if that social setting were to disappear, then one might expect prophecy itself to change in some fundamental way. In other words, there are social prerequisites for prophecy.[10] However, not all social contexts elicit intermediation. And not all intermediation grows out of the same social context.

4. The prophet possesses distinctive personal qualities, for example, charisma. The work of Max Weber has pride of place here.[11] Weber maintained that a personal force, charisma, was the hallmark of prophets. They were imbued with a powerful presence of the holy, which made people pay attention. This spirit (*rûăḥ*) distinguished prophetic authority from that of other religious leaders.

However, Weber's own articulation of the issue has presented problems. Weber maintained that charisma was not simply a psychological quality; rather, it also had a sociological side. Charisma—as charismatic authority, to be distinguished from traditional and from bureaucratic authority—worked itself out by creating a following. One would, therefore, expect a charismatic prophet to attract a group of followers or disciples. This is not always the case with individuals in the Hebrew Bible whom we characterize as prophets. Were we to use Weber's definition, we would, as Dorothy Emmett contends, "have to

---

10 On which see T. Overholt, *Channels of Prophecy: The Social Dynamics of Prophecy* (Minneapolis: Fortress Press, 1989).

11 Weber's analysis about prophets as an ideal type may be found in his *Sociology of Religion* (Boston: Beacon Press, 1964).

restrict the notion of prophet to a type of messianic or millenarian preacher or religious revolutionary. This would be to deny it to many of the kinds of people who are generally known as prophets—the Hebrew prophets, for instance—and this would seem unnatural."[12]

The key issue is the existence of a group of followers around a putative charismatic prophet. Such a group, "the sons of the prophets," is attested in the case of Elisha. There is indication of such a collectivity in Isa 8:16, a text that refers to "my disciples." But apart from that limited evidence, there is little warrant for arguing that Israel's prophets exercised charismatic authority through the creation of a disciple band or some other group gathered around the prophet.

5. *The prophet is an intermediary.* This general notion has been articulated in various ways. James Ross focused on the messenger formula, "thus says the Lord," and deemed the prophets to be messengers—messengers from God to humans.[13] James Muilenburg spoke about the prophets as mediators—individuals, particularly in the covenant context, who stood between the deity and humans.[14] However, we achieve greatest clarity when, using cross-cultural examples, we deem prophets to be intermediaries of a more general sort, those on the boundary between the human and divine worlds. Robert Wilson's and Thomas Overholt's work has been salutary here.[15] The general vocabulary of prophets as intermediaries works beyond the boundaries of the Bible. For those of us interested in placing biblical prophetic literature and behavior within its larger cultural environ, the language of intermediation bears special promise.

One major advantage of adopting the language of intermediary is that it allows one to identify different kinds of intermediaries. This is important because we have prima facie reason to think that there were different kinds of prophets—at Mari, in the Neo-Assyrian texts, and in ancient Israel. In all three settings, we confront labels that hint at different kinds of intermediation. At Mari, the roster includes individuals known as *muhhûm, āpilum, assinnu, nabûm, qam(m)atum,* as well as

---

12 D. Emmett, "Prophets and Their Societies," *JRAS* 86 (1956): 16.

13 J. Ross, "The Prophet as Yahweh's Messenger," in *Prophecy in Israel: Search for an Identity* (ed. D. Petersen; IRT 10; Philadelphia: Fortress Press, 1987), 112–21.

14 J. Muilenburg, "The 'Office' of the Prophet in Ancient Israel," in *The Bible in Modern Scholarship* (ed. J. Hyatt; Nashville: Abingdon Press, 1967), 74–97.

15 R. Wilson, *Prophecy and Society in Ancient Israel* (Philadelphia: Fortress Press, 1980), and Overholt, *Channels of Prophecy.*

private persons. In the Neo-Assyrian corpus, we read about the *raggimu, mahhû,* and *šabrû.* And in the biblical material, we confront the labels *rōʾê, ḥōzê, nābîʾ*, and *ʾîš hāʾĕlōhîm.*

The significance of these labels is open to debate. At this point, I simply suggest that they probably reflect different behaviors.[16] For example, the term *rōʾê* is rooted in a biblical text, 1 Sam 9, which involves something akin to a divination report. This is a different kind of prophetic activity than that associated with Elisha as *ʾîš hāʾĕlōhîm,* when he curses the boys or causes an ax head to float (2 Kgs 2:23–25; 6:1–7). Put simply, intermediation took place through different behaviors, which are themselves reflected in the various labels.

6. The prophet has a distinctive message. Some scholars have maintained that prophets, particularly in Israel, were important because they espoused a distinctive message or theological perspective. The most famous of such claims is surely that of Wellhausen, who maintained that prophets were responsible for articulating "ethical monotheism" in ancient Israel, a new amalgam and high watermark in ethical and theological thought. There has been a swing away from such a notion, particularly in the work of von Rad, who, following E. Rohland, maintained that prophets were recasting earlier traditions rather than forging new ones.[17] The spirit of Wellhausen, however, is alive and well, as is evident from such claims as Koch's, that prophets were responsible for creating "an ethical, futuristic monotheism."[18] Koch speaks as well of the prophets who generated the notion of a "metahistory." "For the first time in the history of mankind, human beings dared to make hope the foundation of their ontology and their theology. The prophets therefore brought a futuristic turn into the thinking of following centuries, a sense of incompleteness and a further purpose to be found in the course of world events."[19] For Koch, the prophets had a distinctive message—they were theological innovators. My own view is that certain prophets may have offered innovative ideas, for example, Isaiah's idea that Yahweh had an overarching

16 See D. Petersen, *The Roles of Israel's Prophets* (JSOTSup 17; Sheffield: JSOT Press, 1981).

17 G. von Rad, *Old Testament Theology* (vol. 2; New York: Harper & Row, 1965).

18 K. Koch, *The Prophets: The Assyrian Period* (Philadelphia: Fortress Press, 1983), 13.

19 Ibid., 163.

plan for the world. Nevertheless, it is difficult to speak of a characteristic prophetic message, whether inside or outside Israel.

More generally accepted are expositions on less grandiose features of prophetic literature. For example, James Mays has argued on behalf of an ethical tradition in the eighth-century prophets regarding justice.[20] Such an argument holds special importance, particularly if one views the prophets are intermediaries. One wishes to know, in a particular cultural setting, if there were "content" in that intermediation or if the prophets could say virtually anything in that process.

•

These then are the primary options—definitions that focus on religious experience, distinctive literature, social setting, personal charisma, the prophet's role as intermediary, and distinctive message. However, only one of these typologics, the notion of prophet as intermediary, seems comprehensive enough to help understand prophets throughout the ancient Near East, including those attested in the Hebrew Bible and in the Old Babylonian and Neo-Assyrian texts.

Recent Definitions

Now it is time to ask: How is recent scholarly discussion related to this typology? As a case in point, I reflect briefly on a dictionary entry, published in the *Neues Bibel-Lexikon* (1997), relevant to discussions of prophecy in Israel and the ancient Near East.[21] In that volume, a prophet is defined as

> [a] person who (*a*) through a cognitive experience (vision, an auditory experience, an audio-visual appearance, a dream or the like) becomes the subject of the revelation of a deity, or several deities and, in addition, (*b*) is conscious of being commissioned by the deity or deities in question to convey the revelation in a verbal form (as a "prophecy" or a "prophetic speech"), or through nonverbal communicative acts ("symbolic acts"), to a third party who constitutes the actual addressee of the message.[22]

---

[20] J. Mays, "Justice: Perspectives from the Prophetic Tradition," in Petersen, *Prophecy in Israel*, 144–58.

[21] M. Weippert, "Prophetie im Alten Orient," *NBL* 197.

[22] This English translation is provided by M. Nissinen, *References to Prophecy in Neo-Assyrian Sources* (SAAS 7; Helsinki: Neo-Assyrian Text Corpus Project, 1998), 5.

This definition appears to reflect one of the types I have just examined, namely, the emphasis on prophets as individuals who had peculiar forms of experience, a view associated with Gunkel and Lindblom. In this recent definition, the experience is described as "cognitive," which presumably means that the experience can be articulated or expressed.

When we reflect on this definition from the perspective of the prior analysis, several problems appear. First, the definition appeals to "experience," not to observable behavior. Unless the experience as such is reported, one has no reason to claim that someone is a prophet. Second, how are we to understand texts or reports that include no references to such experience? For example, what should we think about ARM 26 414, which narrates the activity and words of Atamrum, the *āpilum* of Šamaš? Here we deal with a person who has a down-to-earth message: "Send me a discreet scribe and I will have (him) write down the news which Shamash has sent me for the king."[23] There is no implicit or explicit reference to a distinctive cognitive experience, other than the reference to "the news" that Šamaš had sent. Third, the definition refers to the "conscious[ness] of being commissioned by the deity." Even in the biblical material, only four prophetic books (Isaiah, Jeremiah, Ezekiel, and Amos) offer overt reports about such self-consciousness. (We should note that a number of scholars do not think that these texts reflect the self-understanding of the prophets, but are instead later additions.) Are we then to disallow the rest of the Prophetic Books in the Hebrew Bible, such as Zephaniah or Joel, from being construed as prophetic literature simply because they do not include commissioning narratives or reports about a sense of call? The same may be said for prophetic texts from either Mari or Nineveh. These texts do not routinely report on prophets' consciousness of being called or commissioned by the deity. We should say that some prophetic texts offer evidence of a sense of call, but many do not. Hence, it is risky to define prophets as individuals who possessed this conviction of divine commission.

The definition in the *Neues Bibel-Lexikon* reflects the first category

---

23 H. Huffmon, "The Expansion of Prophecy in the Mari Archives: New Texts, New Readings, New Information," in *Prophecy and Prophets: The Diversity of Contemporary Issues in Scholarship* (ed. Y. Gitay; Semeia Studies; Atlanta: Society of Biblical Literature, 1997), 11.

examined, namely, an individual who has a distinctive form of experience. However, as we have seen, the disadvantage of this concept is that it prevents us from thinking that there were prophets of different sorts, some in states of possession, others not. To be fair, the definition does specify various experiences, for example, vision or audition, which might, in turn, be manifest in diverse behaviors reflected by the different prophetic labels. Still, this carefully constructed definition of "prophet" appears overly monolithic and excessively reliant on the Gunkel and Lindblom heritage concerning biblical prophets.

Prophets and Prophetic Literature

I now propose a relation between the typology of prophets as intermediaries and prophetic literature.[24] I contend simply that prophetic literature reflects different kinds of intermediation. If some prophets experienced states of possession, one would expect the vision report to be a primary form of prophetic literature. If some acted as holy men, one would expect literature celebrating the power of the holy, namely, *legenda,* to be a primary form. And such is the case. Different types of intermediation led to different forms of literature.

When one examines the Israelite material, one discerns at least five basic forms of prophetic literature: divinatory chronicle, vision report, prophetic speech, legend, and prophetic historiography. Let me briefly characterize each. (1) First Samuel 9 offers a case of the *divinatory chronicle,* describing the divinatory activities of someone known as a *rōʾê.* The diviner, Samuel, helps Saul find lost sheep. The report conveys the social process that elicits divination as well as the divinatory utterance. (2) There are numerous examples of *vision reports* in the Hebrew Bible and outside Israel. One should say that prophetic behavior takes place in the creation of the report rather than in the vision, which is itself utterly subjective. It is interesting that books which feature the term *ḥōzê,* "seer" (Amos 7), include reports of visions. This literary form, normally written in prose, effects intermediation since it conveys to the hearer or reader information about the world of the deity. (3) The *prophetic speech,* whether divine oracle or prophetic saying, is the literary manifestation of someone who receives and reports

[24] See also D. Petersen, "Rethinking the Nature of Prophetic Literature," in Gitay, *Prophecy and Prophets,* 23–40.

auditions. Prophetic words as such, often, though not exclusively, in poetic form, are primary. (4) The hagiographic literature of *prophetic legenda* is a direct reflection of a holy man's behavior, of the *ʾîš hāʾĕlōhîm.* This style of literature focuses on the powerful holy in the world of the profane. Biblical literature offers direct evidence of the *Sitz im Leben* that produced such literature, the storytelling environment attested in 2 Kgs 8:4.[25] (5) There is some evidence of *prophetic historiography,* in which prophets are viewed as individuals who act as scribes (1 Chr 29:29). Moreover, a number of scholars have pointed to a level of redaction in Deuteronomistic history that seems to reflect the world of the prophets, namely, one in which the prophetic word has special power (e.g., 1 Kgs 12:15). Prophets who wrote from this perspective created historiographic literature.

We may make the same sorts of claims when we examine the Neo-Assyrian material. For example, one would expect the behavior of the "shouter," the *raggimu,* to result in either speeches or reports of public encounter. Those kinds of literature are, in fact, prominent in the Neo-Assyrian corpus. More generally, that corpus includes both oracular collections and references to prophetic activity in texts such as royal inscriptions.[26] We may conclude that, both in Israel and in the larger ancient Near Eastern environ, different forms of prophetic literature stem from diverse forms of intermediation.

Mesopotamian and Israelite Prophecy

It is not the purpose of this essay to compare biblical and ancient Near Eastern texts systematically. Other essays in this volume have that as their agenda. However, the material published by Simo Parpola has made me conscious of two things. First, the number of prophetic labels in the Neo-Assyrian period is much smaller than it had been at Mari. The term *raggimu* by the Neo-Assyrian period had become normative. Other terms—*mahhû, assinnu, āpiltu*—had fallen out of use. As a biblical scholar, I find this case strikingly similar to the prominence that the term *nābîʾ* achieves in ancient Israel. Over time, it too becomes normative, with *ḥōzê, rōʾê,* and *ʾîš hāʾĕlōhîm* becoming far less

[25] On which see A. Rofé, *The Prophetical Stories: The Narratives about the Prophets in the Hebrew Bible, Their Literary Types and History* (Jerusalem: Magnes, 1988).

[26] S. Parpola, *Assyrian Prophecies* (SAA 9; Helsinki: Helsinki University Press, 1997), liii.

prominent. One wonders what linguistic or social forces were at work for this process to occur both in the Levant and Mesopotamia.

Second, the Neo-Assyrian prophetic texts are important for understanding the formation of prophetic literature. At Mari, individual texts were archived. There is minimal, if any, evidence of integrating various oracles or reports. In contrast, at Nineveh, individual oracles were integrated into collections. Such archival and editorial activity permits—for the first time with prophetic literature outside the Bible—examination of what biblical scholars have labeled redaction criticism. This is one of the most fascinating aspects of the Neo-Assyrian materials. It is striking that such collecting may have been going on in both Israel and Nineveh at about the same time—with Amos and La-dagil-ili. A number of questions arise. What was the Israelite analog to the *ṭuppu* format, in which several oracles were collected? Why in Israel were the sayings of one prophet combined whereas, in Nineveh, the collections included the oracles of different individuals? Collection One (SAA 9 1), for example, includes oracles from ten individuals, eight of whom are named. In Collection One, no individual is represented by more than one oracle. This is not because only one oracle per individual was part of the tradition. For example, the sayings of La-dagil-ili are preserved in the first, second, and third collections. Although he is mentioned only once in the third collection (SAA 9 3), it may be that more than one of the oracles in that collection stems from him.

If the biblical collections focus on one named individual, the Neo-Assyrian collections are, according to Parpola, oriented around chronological and thematic issues. The most overtly unified collection, the third, reflects the making of a covenant, along with its implications. Collection One appears to offer oracles and reports that reflect on a military campaign and its successful conclusion; Collection Two (SAA 9 2) offers oracles concerning the initial political problems that attended Esarhaddon's accession. Is it too much to suggest that similar collections may have existed early in the formation of Israel's prophetic literature? Amos 1–2 seems to offer an analog, as might the woe oracles in Isa 1–39.

Summary

In this essay, I have charted ways one might understand prophets. In that regard, I have argued, consistent with scholarly perspectives of the last third of the twentieth century, that prophets should be understood as intermediaries who acted in different ways, as various prophetic labels suggest. Further, I have related the forms of intermediation, as reflected in the specific labels both in Israel and in the larger ancient Near Eastern context, to types of prophetic literature, both biblical and extrabiblical. I have suggested that the recent publication of Neo-Assyrian prophetic texts may help gain new perspective on the formation of prophetic collections in ancient Israel. Such analysis contributes to our understanding of prophetic behavior both in Israel and in the ancient Near East, along with the literature that derives from that behavior.

Part Two

STUDIES IN SOURCES

4

A Company of Prophets: Mari, Assyria, Israel

Herbert B. Huffmon

"A rose is a rose is a rose is a rose" is the most widely cited line by the American writer Gertrude Stein, but by this saying—printed as a motto on her notepaper—she demonstrates her subversive, experimental attitude toward the rules of language and writing.[1] Stein is not intending to offer a botanical observation that all roses are the same. And when we shift from flowers to people, in particular to the religious roles of various individuals, we cannot say, identifying all as one, "a priest is a priest is a priest is a priest." Priests are not all the same, and priests in ancient Egypt or Mesopotamia are not the same as priests in ancient Israel or in the Christian church, although there are overlapping roles. Nor can we say, by way of identification, "a prophet is a prophet is a prophet is a prophet." In the "company" of prophets in the ancient Near East there are many "subsidiaries," so to speak, sharing commonalities but engaging in distinctive practices and contributing in different ways to the religious life of their communities.

Wilfred Cantwell Smith has downplayed the importance of analyzing the "plain" phenomenological data among religious systems or traditions, such as comparing the design and architectural placement of altars, which we might call the "manifestation" aspect of religion. Rather, Smith emphasizes "the role of those data in the lives of the persons concerned."[2] This emphasis more closely approximates what we might call the "essence" or "meaning" of the religious activity, as emphasized by the phenomenologists of religion. The point is illustrated by Smith's contention that the familiar proposition, "the Qur'an is to Islam as the Bible is to Christianity," though in no way absurd, is an oversimplification that should be supplemented by the proposition

[1] On this phrase, see Gertrude Stein's *Autobiography of Alice B. Toklas* (Week-End Library ed.; London: John Lane, 1935), 184–85.

[2] W. C. Smith, *On Understanding Islam: Selected Studies* (Religion and Reason 19; The Hague, Paris, and New York: Mouton, 1981), 233.

that "the Qurʾan is to Islam as the person of Jesus Christ is to Christianity."[3] He illustrates this point elsewhere by his suggestion that, rather than the role of Jesus, the role of the apostle Paul in Christianity is most comparable to the role of Muḥammad in Islam.[4] In accordance with this perspective, this essay attempts to sketch not only the phenomenological similarities but also the different contextual roles of prophets from Mari, Assyria, and Israel.

In the royal archives of Mari, the Neo-Assyrian texts, and the Hebrew Bible, together with related texts, we find a commonality in distinctive settings and with differing manifestations. The commonality is that prophets (1) present communications from the divine world, normally for a third party, and serve as mediators who may or may not identify with the deity; (2) draw upon inspiration through ecstasy, dreams, or what may be called "inner illumination"; (3) offer messages, often unsolicited, that are immediately understandable by the audience addressed; and (4) not only offer assurance but frequently admonish or exhort the addressee. This prophetic activity, however, takes place within different contexts and develops in different ways. Within each community the prophets are perceived in different ways by different people, reflecting the particular settings and perspectives of those involved.

Mari

The royal archives of Mari of the eighteenth century B.C.E., in addition to two ritual texts that mention prophets,[5] tell about prophetic activity in approximately fifty of some eight thousand letters[6] and in

---

[3] Ibid., 238–39.

[4] W. C. Smith, *Islam in Modern History* (Princeton: Princeton University Press, 1957), 17–18, n. 13.

[5] Jean-Marie Durand and Michaël Guichard, "Les rituels de Mari," in *Florilegium marianum III: Recueil d'études à la mémoire de Marie-Thérèse Barrelet* (ed. D. Charpin and J.-M. Durand; Mémoires de *NABU* 4; Paris: SEPOA, 1997), 19–63.

[6] Jean-Marie Durand, *Archives épistolaires de Mari* I/1 (ARM 26; Paris: Éditions Recherche sur les Civilisations, 1988). Note also Dominique Charpin et al., *Archives épistolaires de Mari* I/2 (ARM 26; Paris: Éditions Recherche sur les Civilisations, 1988). Reference to Mari texts will be by edition number in ARM 26, unless otherwise indicated. For A. 1121+, see Bertrand Lafont, "Le roi de Mari et les prophètes de dieu Adad," *RA* 78 (1984): 7–18; for A. 1968, see Jean-Marie Durand, "Le mythologème de combat entre le dieu de l'orage et la mer en Mésopotamie," *MARI* 7 (1993): 41–61.

about twelve of some twelve thousand economic and administrative texts.[7] Prophetic activity is sparsely reported. These reports, however, come from as far away as Aleppo in the west and Babylon in the east, and identify the speakers by a variety of titles. The titles that occur most frequently are *āpilum/āpiltum*, "answerer," and *muhhûm/muhhūtum*, "ecstatic." The less-frequent titles are *assinnum*, "cult singer," and *nabû*, "ones called," and the title *qammātum* is of uncertain translation.[8] These titles are provided by the correspondents and represent the community's identification of these individuals' roles; the titles are not given as self-reference. There is one letter (194), however, in which the *āpilum*, "answerer," of Šamaš identifies himself as the sender and mentions another [*āpi*] *lum*. Many who convey messages from the gods, however, are not identified by a prophetic title, although they may be prominent persons in the royal court. Some may be a "chief temple administrator" (*šangû*).

Also impressive is the array of deities mentioned: the *āpilum/āpiltum* speaks for the gods Addu, Addu of Halab, Addu of Kallassu, Dagan, Dagan of Tuttul, Dagan of Subatum, Marduk, Nergal, and Šamaš, and for the affiliated goddesses Annunitum, Diritum, and Hišametum; the *assinnum* speaks for Annunitum; the *muhhûm/muhhūtum* speaks for the gods Addu, Amu of Hubšalum/Nergal, Dagan, Dagan of Terqa, Dagan of Tuttul, and Itur-Mer, and for the goddesses Annunitum, Ištar, Ištar of Irradan, and Ninhursagga/Šala(š); the *qammātum* is connected with Dagan of Terqa. The prophets without title are connected with the goddesses Annunitum, Belet-biri, and Belet-ekallim, and the gods Dagan, Dagan of Terqa, and Itur-Mer. The prophets are widely dispersed and connected with a similarly wide range of deities.

These prophetic messages are taken seriously by the political authorities, but they are not the first or preferred means of communicating with the gods. Prophetic messages are clearly subordinate to other, more common means of divine communication. The messages, in the

---

[7] Jean-Marie Durand, "Les prophéties des textes de Mari," in *Oracles et prophéties dans l'antiquité: Actes du colloque de Strasbourg, 15–17 Juin 1995* (ed. J.-G. Heintz; Université des sciences humaines de Strasbourg, Travaux du Centre de recherche sur le Proche-Orient et la Grèce antiques 15; Paris: De Boccard, 1997), 115–34, esp. 115–16. See also the list compiled by Martti Nissinen in this volume, 90, n. 8.

[8] Although *nabû* is cognate with Hebrew *nābîʾ*, the precise meaning of the term in the Mari text (ARM 26 216) is unclear. Durand (ReS 333–34, 451) now allows that *qammātum* (ARM 26 197; 199; 203), which may refer to a particular hairstyle, could be a personal name rather than a title.

absence of personal communication (for which there are only indirect hints), are reported in letters to the king. In this official communication, the messengers are subject to review by technical divination, normally by extispicy, but on occasion by other means, whether through sickness (a sign of being touched by the divine), the offering of sacrifice, or trustworthiness (ARM 26 233:53). The letters report frequently that, either voluntarily or as a requirement, the prophets submit a bit of their hair (*šārtum*) and a trimming from their garment (*sissiktum*)—the hair and hem. This happens with all categories of prophet: *āpilum* (two or three times), *muhhûm* (twice), *assinnum* (twice), *qammātum* (once), and untitled prophets (six times, once with the hair and hem omitted). Another sign of subordination is that the prophets at times complain that their previous messages have been ignored.

The "hair and hem" are surely used as technical divination, as a means of verifying the authenticity of the prophetic word. In ARM 26 182, a man who does not receive a clear answer by means of technical *bārûm*-divination sends his hair and hem to the king for a response from the court's *bārûm*-diviners. Once (ARM 26 204:16–18), an *āpiltum* says of her hair and hem, "Let them [the materials or the diviners] clear/purify [me—from guilt/fault]" (*lizakkû*). In another Mari text (ARM 26 215:25), the king's correspondent advises, regarding the hair and hem of a *muhhûm*, "Let my lord make purification" (*lizakki*). An Old Babylonian text from Karana (Tell al-Rimah) tells about a sick man whose hair and hem were submitted to technical divination, which cleared him of "sin/guilt" in connection with his illness.[9] Similarly, in the *tamītu* texts, the person for whom the divinatory question was submitted could be represented by "a piece of the fringe of his garment or of his fingernail."[10]

Another indication of the messages' secondary status is that they were subject to review before being communicated to the king. The king's correspondent, Queen Šiptu, in some instances examined the prophetic message by special divination involving drink; by putting a question with reference to an *assinnum* ("for five days," or, "on the fifth

---

[9] Stephanie Dalley et al., *The Old Babylonian Tablets from Tell al Rimah* ([London:] British School of Archaeology in Iraq, 1976), no. 65, pp. 64–65.

[10] W. G. Lambert, "The 'tamītu' Texts," in *La divination en Mésopotamie ancienne et dans les régions voisines* (CRRAI 14; Paris: Presses Universitaires de France, 1966), 120–21; idem, "Questions Addressed to the Babylonian Oracle: The *tamītu* Texts," in Heintz, *Oracles et propheties*, 85–98, esp. 91–92.

day"; ARM 26 212); by investigating "'signs,' male and female" (ARM 26 207); and by getting a favorable answer regarding the king and an unfavorable answer regarding the king's enemy. Verification is also sought for a number of dream messages (ARM 26 82; 142; 225; 229; 239), and sometimes, the correspondent notes, confirmation was not attained (ARM 26 142; A. 1121+).

In three texts, the king's correspondent, having reported a prophetic message, advises him not to proceed without extispicy, that is, technical divination (ARM 26 204, involving an *āpiltum;* ARM 26 217, coming from an unidentified woman; ARM 26 239, a princess's dream). In A. 1968, reporting on an *āpilum* of Addu of Aleppo, the prophet himself advises King Zimri-Lim not to depart without a (favorable) omen, presumably referring to an extispicy.[11] Yet we also find, in ARM 26 199, that Lupahum, an *āpilum* of Dagan, is dispatched by the king to Dagan of Tuttul to inquire about a report that the king had received. The *āpilum* obtained a report and went to Der (in the Mari area), to which he had gone previously, bearing a gift and a warning for the goddess Diritum about her trust in Ešnunna. He then gave the king's correspondent a message supporting a cautious policy toward Ešnunna, a policy the king subsequently rejected.

The prophets are both male and female. Among the references to the higher-status "answerers" (*āpilū),* the men predominate, with a ratio of about sixteen-to-two; one of the men—counted once—is cited in three different texts. Among the references to the "ecstatics" (*muhhû),* the men predominate by a lesser margin, about twenty- or twenty-one-to-eight, although the nature of the references does not allow a precise count. The two "cult singers" (*assinnū*) are "male," whether intact or castrates, and there are three references to a *qammātum*—perhaps the same person—if this is viewed as a title and not a personal name. References to the prophets as a group—*āpilū, muhhû,* and to some *nabû*—occasionally might intend to include women as well as men. Among persons not identified by one of the prophetic titles, the gender distribution is much more even, about nine-to-ten, with men in a slight minority.[12]

---

[11] See Dominique Charpin, "Le context historique et géographique des prophèties dans les textes retrouvés à Mari," *BCSMS* 23 (1992): 21–31, esp. 29–30; for the text, see Durand, "Mythologème de combat," 44–45, lines 12'–13'.

[12] This count includes the text published by Claus Wilcke ("Dagan-nahmis Traum," *WO* 17 [1986]: 11–16), which presumably comes from Mari and dates to

In giving messages the prophets appear individually, although in one dream message (ARM 26 227), a woman, whose name is only partly preserved, reports that she saw two deceased "ecstatics" (*muhhû*) who had a joint message for the king. "Ecstatics" speak in ARM 26 243, and another text refers to "five [*muh*]*hû* of Addu,"[13] but the clearest indication of group activity is the Hanaean *nabû* gathered to respond to an inquiry from the king (ARM 26 216) in the fashion of divinatory questions asked by the *bārû*-diviner (and reminiscent of 1 Kgs 22). In addition, ARM 27 32 refers to "ecstatics" of the god Amu (of) Hubšalum, who may also have been (or accompanied) elders of the town of Gaššum on their way to see the king; this group seized four men of Yamutbal and took them to a regional official, but this is not reported as ritual or oracular activity.

Those given the prophetic titles *āpilum/āpiltum* ("answerer"), *muhhûm/muhhūtum* ("ecstatic"), and *qammātum*, if a title, were cultic personnel, although not priests who officiated in the sacrificial or general cultus. Rather, they were part of the temple entourage that specialized in verbal communication from the deity. The *assinnum* ("cult singer") is well attested elsewhere as a cult functionary associated with Ištar and her congeners, and engaged in singing, dancing, ecstasy, and perhaps cross-dressing, but in the Mari context the *assinnum*'s role may have been more restricted.[14] The title *āpilum/āpiltum*, "answerer," implies providing an answer to a query, although a *muhhūtum* advises the king that "I will continue to answer" (*ātanappal*, ARM 26 237:26). The title *muhhûm/muhhūtum*, "ecstatic," points to the process through which answers are received, and, indeed, one of the Ištar ritual texts refers to the *muhhûm* becoming ecstatic, as confirmed in one of the letters.[15] Others are cited as "becoming ecstatic," namely, Šelibum, an *assinnum*

---

the time of the main Mari archives (see Durand, *Archives*, 462–63, n. 49), although it is not from the Mari excavations. The text reports on an offering prompted by a dream, but the dream itself is not reported. The name of the dreamer, who is male, occurs as a feminine name in ARM 10 116.

13 For the reference to five [*muh*]*hûs* of Addu, see G. Ozan, "Les lettres de Manatan," in Charpin and Durand, *Florilegium marianum III*, 303, no. 152:5 (= M. 9451).

14 See Stefan M. Maul, "*Kurgarrû* und *assinnu* und ihr Stand in der babylonischen Gesellschaft," in *Außenseiter und Randgruppen: Beiträge zu einer Sozialgeschichte des Alten Orients* (ed. V. Haas; Xenia: Konstanzer Althistorische Vorträge und Forschungen 32; Konstanz, Germany: Universitätsverlag, 1992), 159–71.

15 For the Ištar ritual, see Durand and Guichard, "Rituels de Mari," 53–54, lines ii.23', 26'; note that the Irra-gamil who becomes ecstatic in ARM 26 222 is identified as a *muhhûm* in ARM 21 333:34' and 23 446:9'.

(ARM 26 213; cf. 197, 198), and Ahatum, a young (servant?) woman (ARM 26 214), both in the temple of Annunitum.

The *āpilum*, who had a somewhat higher status among the prophets, and the *muhhûm* are associated even by their titles with providing messages from the gods. Their messages are also frequently connected with sacrifice or other temple event, at which time the prophet "arises and speaks." When these prophets convey a complaint to the king, the complaint often refers to royal neglect of the deity's cult or cultic property (ARM 26 220; 221; A. 1121+; A. 1968; etc.). Presumably, the Hanaean *nabû* group was also associated with the cultus. Many messages, however, derive from persons without a prophetic title—speakers identified by name, residence, or status. Many such messages derive from the women of the Mari court. Strikingly, a *šangû*, "chief temple administrator," reports a revelatory dream (ARM 26 238); another *šangû* speaks in one of the dreams of the queen mother, Adduduri (ARM 26 237); and a third *šangû* reports to Queen Šiptu, the king's correspondent, on a young woman's dream (ARM 26 214).[16]

Virtually all of the messages are addressed to the king—we are dealing with the royal archives, after all. But on occasion the message addresses local people concerning what they should do. The letter ARM 26 221-bis, from the king's representative in Terqa, reports that a *muhhûm* addressed him regarding (re)building a gate, the second request cast clearly in the plural, as if addressed to the people of Terqa or at least to the "governor" and his workers (lines 23–30): "[If (?)] you (pl.) do not build that gate, [a cal]amity (?) will occur. You (pl.) are [no]t getting anywhere. [Thi]s is what that *muhhûm* [sai]d to me. But I am [eng]aged with the ha[r]v[est]. To turn ov[er] my [ser]vants, I cannot do." On another occasion the *muhhûm* spoke to a public audience (ARM 26 216), presumably with the intent of putting pressure on the king to order various cities to return sacred items. The correspondent notes that this message was delivered "in the assembly of the elders." Other messages are delivered at the temple gate, where presumably the public would also be present.

The prophetic messages typically assure the king of success or warn of possible dangers. At times, however, the prophets express concern

16 Note the Ishchali texts from the archive of the *šangûs* of the Kititum temple, in which the goddess Kititum addresses the king, Ibal-pi-El, directly (Maria deJong Ellis, "The Goddess Kititum Speaks to King Ibalpiel: Oracle Texts from Ishchali," *MARI* 5 [1987]: 235–66).

that certain cultic acts, such as special sacrifices, have been neglected (ARM 26 220; 221; 231; see also ARM 26 224). But the prophet may also raise—even repeatedly (having done so five times previously)—issues of cult property (A. 1121+). Requests for regular information also occur (Dagan of Terqa, 233). All of these requests are represented as being in the king's self-interest (e.g., ARM 26 194; 217; 218; 219; 227). Consistent with acting in the king's self-interest, prophets are mentioned in several administrative texts as having received gifts or supplies from the king. An *āpilum* is mentioned several times as having received a garment, bronze nails, silver ring, and a donkey distributed from booty; a *muhhûm* receives clothing and jewelry; a *qammātum* receives a garment and nose ring. One *muhhûm* receives a silver ring "when he gave the message to the king" (ARM 25 142:12–15; see Durand, *Archives*, 380). Sometimes the prophets request these gifts directly (e.g., ARM 26 199; 206).

Contrasted with these modest incursions into the king's realm, however, is the special assertiveness of the *āpilum*-prophets of Addu of Aleppo/Kallassu. Speaking from the historical dominance of the Aleppo kingdom in the life of Zimri-Lim and his family, and within the protection of an independent jurisdiction, a series of messages reminds Zimri-Lim, "What I have given I can take away," and makes specific requests (A. 1121+). The Mari representative, seemingly embarrassed by the message, appeals to his traditional duty to convey information about what others are doing and saying about the king, and notes the warnings that might lead to future disasters if ignored. The same letter reports an admonition from Addu to the king of Mari, "When a plaintiff, male or female, makes an appeal to you, take note and give them justice," together with an assurance of benefits for an attentive king. Another letter from Zimri-Lim's representative in Aleppo (A. 1968), again citing the beneficence that Addu has shown the king, adds, "Whenever anyone with a claim cries out to <you>, saying, 'I have been w[rong]ed,' stand up and decide his case; ans[wer him] [fai]rly" (lines 7'–10'). Addu reminds the Mari king that he is subject to a higher authority, parallel to the slightly later epilogue of the Laws of Hammurapi, "In order that the mighty not wrong the weak, to provide just ways for the waif and the widow, I have inscribed my precious pronouncements upon my stele . . . to provide just ways for the wronged." The Laws add, "Let the wronged man who has a lawsuit come before the statue of me, the king of justice. . . . let my stele reveal the lawsuit for him; may he examine his case, may he calm his heart. . . ."[17]

Another sign of assertiveness appears in a letter (ARM 26 194) apparently sent from Northeast Syria (Jebel Sinjar area) by the *āpilum* of Šamaš. This *āpilum* seems to serve as a clearinghouse for distant requests of deities (from Sippar to the southeast to Aleppo to the west), possibly from within a council of the gods or as a cult functionary associated with various deities.[18] Insisting on direct communication by bypassing the king's representative, the *āpilum* demands a "safeguarded" scribe (ARM 26 414; granting, following Durand, that this letter is connected with ARM 26 194) and submits a multitude of requests—for a throne and a royal daughter to Sippar; taboo items for Addu of Aleppo; a gift for Dagan; items, including a sword, for Nergal, king of Hubšalum. The list concludes with the assurance of perpetual kingship for Zimri-Lim and a request that the king "sen[d] to my feet (anyone with a) [cl]aim."

Most striking is a *muhhûm* of Dagan's dramatic action. The *muhhûm* asks for a lamb and proceeds to eat it, raw, in public—reminiscent of the Sumerian stereotype of the Amorite who "eats uncooked meat."[19] Thereupon the *muhhûm* requests widespread cultic restitution and adds, "For the well-being of your Lord, Zi[mri-Lim], clothe me with a garment" (ARM 26 206:23–24). The king's correspondent provides him with a garment. In another text, a *qammātum*, or the Lady Qammatum of Dagan of Terqa, having warned the king about proceeding in peace negotiations with Ešnunna (ARM 26 199), requests and receives a garment and a nose ring. In stronger fashion, Dagan's prophetic voices opposed, in Zimri-Lim's sixth year—following a year or more of warfare—his conclusion of a treaty with Ešnunna. The situation is clarified by examining the extensive correspondence on the relationship between Mari and Ešnunna. Promising victory for Zimri-

---

[17] Martha T. Roth, *Law Collections from Mesopotamia and Asia Minor* (SBLWAW 6; Atlanta: Scholars Press, 1995), 133–34 (xlvii 59–78), 134 (xlviii 3–19).

[18] Regarding the divine council, see Abraham Malamat, "The Secret Council and Prophetic Involvement in Mari and Israel," in *Prophetie und geschichtliche Wirklichkeit im alten Israel: Festschrift für Siegfried Herrmann* (ed. R. Liwak and S. Wagner; Stuttgart: Kohlhammer, 1991), 231–36. Note also that cultic personnel could be affiliated with a number of deities, even within a given temple, which honors a primary deity and affiliated deities.

[19] See Samuel Noah Kramer, *The Sumerians, Their History, Culture, and Character* (Chicago: University of Chicago Press, 1963), 253.

Lim, Lupahum, an *āpilum* of Dagan who had arrived from Tuttul, as well as a *qammātum* of Dagan of Terqa—apparently independent of each other, although reported in the same letter—oppose an agreement between Mari and Ešnunna, advising that Ešnunna is not trustworthy. The *qammātum* says, "Water runs under the straw" (ARM 26 197; 199; see also 202 for the same phrase from a *muhhûm*).[20] The same *āpilum*, Lupahum, warns the goddess Diritum in Der (Mari area) not to trust Ešnunna. This is an example of different gods, that is, different temple communities, promoting conflicting policies, although both surely represented themselves as acting in the best interests of the king. The difference, however, is aired without direct polemic. Zimri-Lim, on his part, made the treaty with Ešnunna, acknowledging Ešnunna as his superior.[21] In all this prophetic activity, however, it is important to remember Durand's observation that the prophecies are intended "to properly channel the royal power, not to challenge it."[22]

The prophet's inspiration is not always indicated. Between fifteen and twenty—depending on which texts one includes—receive their message in a dream, with one text referring to incubation (ARM 26 232). At least six revelations take place within a temple, or the person goes to a temple in a dream. The presence of the divine, a special "state of consciousness," may be indicated by the prophet's sickness (ARM 26 371). Several times the message states that a deity "sent" the prophet (messenger) or the message (*assinnum*, ARM 26 212; *muhhûm*, ARM 26 220; 221; untitled person, ARM 26 210; 233; 240), and an *āpilum* refers to "the message which Šamaš sent me for the king" (ARM 26 414). Ecstasy itself is mentioned five times—once for an *assinnum*, twice for a *muhhûm* (including the reference in an Ištar ritual), twice for private women. Such inspiration is suggested in the many references in which the prophet "got up" (*itbe*), often in the temple and in connection with sacrifice, and spoke (as "answerer," six times; as "ecstatic," twice), and is associated especially with Ištar and her associates.

---

20 On this proverb, see Jack M. Sasson, "Water beneath Straw: Adventures of a Prophetic Phrase in the Mari Archives," in *Solving Riddles and Untying Knots: Biblical, Epigraphic, and Semitic Studies in Honor of Jonas C. Greenfield* (ed. A. Zevit, S. Gitin, and M. Sokoloff; Winona Lake, Ind.: Eisenbrauns, 1995), 599–608, who finds the proverb enigmatic, which seems contrary to the context.

21 See Charpin, "Context historique et geographique," 22–25.

22 Durand, *Archives*, 410.

Neo-Assyria

Surprisingly, of the Neo-Assyrian prophetic texts, the most important individual tablet was published in 1875 and made available to noncuneiformists in English translation in 1878; two other major texts were published in 1893, six years prior to the publication of the Wen-Amun text in 1899. Yet the Neo-Assyrian texts were almost systematically neglected until the late 1960s, in spite of reminders of their existence.[23]

The Neo-Assyrian prophetic texts are not only from the Neo-Assyrian period. They are also written in literary Neo-Assyrian, which did not add to their accessibility to scholars. These texts reflect a more narrow range in titles and geography than is the case for the Mari evidence. None of the titles known from Mari occurs in the oracle texts, which use, rather, the specifically Neo-Assyrian term *raggimu/raggintu*, "proclaimer," with some prophecies ascribed to a *šēlūtu*, "votaress." However, the title *maḫḫû*, "ecstatic," a variant of Mari *muḫḫûm*, is used as an alternate term for *raggimu* in Esarhaddon's inscriptions not written in "pure" Neo-Assyrian, and the terms *raggimu* and *maḫḫû* are joined in the Esarhaddon succession treaty.[24] Again, as generally in the Mari texts, the titles do not occur as a self-reference.

Collections SAA 9 1–2 of the prophet reports identify the speakers by name and place of residence. Possibly because she breaks with the pattern of the Ištar affiliates, one speaker is identified by title as a votaress (*šēlūtu*) of the king (SAA 9 1.7). Another text identifies a prophetic speaker as a *šēlūtu*-votaress of Ištar of Arbela.[25] Collection

---

23 For the process of discovery and publication, see Simo Parpola, *Assyrian Prophecies* (SAA 9; Helsinki: Helsinki University Press, 1997), xiii–xiv. Note also the attention given to some of these texts as a potentially separate category by Morris Jastrow (*Religion Babyloniens und Assyriens* [vol. 2/1; Giessen, Germany: Töpelmann, 1912], 156–74, esp. 158). Bruno Meissner writes that some of the texts showed that "es im Zweistromlande ähnlich wie im alten Israel auch Propheten gegeben [hat], die ohne Zuhilfenahme der Wahrsagekunst lediglich durch göttliche Eingebungen die Zukunft verkündeten" (*Babylonien und Assyrien* [vol. 2; Heidelberg: Carl Winter, 1925], 281, but cf. 243). Some of the oracles were available in standard handbooks, but they otherwise remained ignored.

24 Parpola, *Assyrian Prophecies*, xlv–xlvi; Simo Parpola and Kazuko Watanabe, *Neo-Assyrian Treaties and Loyalty Oaths* (SAA 2; Helsinki: Helsinki University Press, 1988), 33.

25 Steven W. Cole and Peter Machinist, *Letters from Priests to the Kings Esarhaddon and Assurbanipal* (SAA 13; Helsinki: Helsinki University Press, 1998), no. 148.

SAA 9 3 is apparently assigned to someone whose name seems lost, with only a portion of the last sign preserved—[. . . DI]NGIR, boldly restored by Parpola as [La-dagil-i]li—but who is identified as a *raggimu*, "proclaimer," of [Arbel]a who speaks for the national god, Aššur, as well as Ištar of Arbela (SAA 9 3.5 iv 31–32). A long individual prophecy report derives from a *raggintu* (SAA 9 7). In other texts of the Neo-Assyrian period, however, there are a number of occurrences of the title *raggimu/raggintu*, including one in which the king provides temporary quarters to a *raggimu* named Quqî.[26] The gender distribution is dominated by women: twelve female prophets and five to six male prophets, plus one or two of uncertain gender.

The prophetic texts are also more concentrated in the deities involved. Front and center is the powerful goddess Ištar of Arbela, seconded by a closely parallel deity, Mullissu (Ninlil), wife of Aššur (Enlil). The two are identified in SAA 9 2.4 ii 30, "The word of Ištar of Arbela, the word of Queen Mullissu," and the two also are linked in SAA 9 5, 7 (". . . his mother is Mullissu . . . his [dry] nurse is the Lady of Arbela," r. 6), and 9. The national god, Aššur, is cited as the oracular source only in SAA 9 3, in which he plays a prominent role together with Ištar of Arbela. One prophecy, from a speaker identified as both male and female—presumably by scribal error but possibly, as Parpola suggests, for a gender-neutral person—speaks for Bel (Marduk), Ištar of Arbela, and Nabu (SAA 9 1.4). This multiple representation is reminiscent of the Mari letter ARM 26 194, but may reflect a cultic functionary associated with several deities or a speaker admitted to the divine council with its multiple voices.[27]

The Neo-Assyrian prophets, like the Mari prophets, were taken seriously by the royal court—in this case Esarhaddon and Assurbanipal, the primary addressees. These prophets seem to have had easy access to the royal court, and there is no evidence for a process of verification. Another indication of the messages' high standing is that the report texts focus solely and immediately on the divine words, unlike the Mari letters in which the king's correspondent often advises him of the prophetic message as one of several news items. The Assyrian texts may begin, "The word of Ištar of Arbela . . ." (SAA 9 5:1), "Ištar of

---

26 F. M. Fales and J. N. Postgate, *Imperial Administrative Records, Part I* (SAA 7; Helsinki: Helsinki University Press, 1992), no. 9 r. i 23.

27 Parpola, *Assyrian Prophecies*, xviii–xxvi, il.

Arbe[la] has said . . ." (SAA 9 6:1), or "The *raggintu*-prophetess . . . (has said)" (SAA 9 7:1)—reports that provide no context apart from what can be reconstructed from the prophecies themselves. Furthermore, more than two-thirds of the Assyrian prophecies are preserved as part of collection tablets, a secondary stage that involved the royal scriptorium—perhaps even one specific scribe—gathering five to six or even ten or more prophetic oracles (or sets of oracles, e.g., SAA 9 1.6) onto one archival tablet. The prophecies were copied for posterity, as they might have been in view of the emphasis on reassurance to the royal family, with only a rare complaint of neglect by the deity mixed in (e.g., SAA 9 3.5). The prophecies were gathered and transferred as a body to individual collection tablets, and thereby were incorporated into the official archives. In this collection process there is also evidence of scribal redaction. For example, in the standardized attribution in collection SAA 9 1, seven times (as preserved) one reads the phrase "from the mouth of so-and-so of such-and-such a place"; however, once, as mentioned, the slight variant occurs for a different category of speaker, "from the mouth of so-and-so, the *šēlūtu*-votaress of the king." The other speakers may have been identified as a category in the first lines of the tablet, now lost.

The pattern of individual messages is broken only by allusions, such as the letter in which Bel-ušezib, a prominent astrologer, asks the king why he had summoned *raggimānu* and *raggimātu*, "prophets and prophetesses," to assist in understanding and dealing with the troubles he had reported. But the writer's chief question seems to be, "Why has the king . . . not summoned me?"[28] He seems to be saying that he would have been more effective than the prophets, even if they may have been present as a group.

The assertive role of the *raggimu* is emphasized in the collection of prophetic oracles reporting on a symbolic treaty commitment by the national god, Aššur, promising victory in battle for king Esarhaddon. The oracle, SAA 9 3.3, is (written down and) deposited in the temple in the presence of the gods; also included is divine vengeance against the enemies of Esarhaddon, who had cried out to Aššur for help. The written covenant is also presented to the king, with full ritual. At the

28 Parpola, *Letters from Assyrian and Babylonian Scholars* (SAA 10; Helsinki: Helsinki University Press, 1993), no. 109 (*ABL* 1216); Martti Nissinen, *References to Prophecy in Neo-Assyrian Sources* (SAAS 7; Helsinki: Neo-Assyrian Text Corpus Project, 1998), 89–95.

initiative of Ištar of Arbela, a covenant meal is then carried out symbolically, with provision for reminders to those who have sworn loyalty to the king, that they might "remember me (Ištar) and keep this covenant which I have made on behalf of Esarhaddon" (SAA 9 3.4 iii 13–15). The collection concludes with Ištar's charge of neglect by Esarhaddon and her reminder of her continuing protection of the king. The concluding attribution assigns the speech to a *raggimu*, presumably from [Arbel]a. Parpola's restoration of the prophet's name as the otherwise attested La-dagil-ili is a bold but plausible restoration.

Apart from the prophecy reports, which provide limited information about the context, there are a number of letters that tell about prophetic activity. These letters show that the prophets were involved in matters affecting the kingship. In one letter, a *raggintu* who had already taken the king's clothes to Babylonia prophesied about removing a throne from the temple for use in a ritual elsewhere that would be beneficial for king Esarhaddon, but the king's representative would not release the throne without the king's permission.[29] This *raggintu* is perhaps the same *raggintu* mentioned in another letter, who, prior to the death and burial of a substitute king, reportedly prophesied to the substitute king—himself apparently of high standing—that he would take over the kingship, that is, that the substitute king would serve in successfully diverting danger from Esarhaddon.[30]

The inscriptions of Assurbanipal include the often-cited reference to a *šabrû*, a "visionary, a seer of dreams," who had a revelation from Ištar of Arbela in which he saw and heard her assure the king that she would fight his battle (against Elam), and that the king could relax and await her victory.[31] But the *šabrû* does not speak directly for the deity.

Throughout, with the exception of a few requests for cultic atten-

29 SAA 13 37; see also Simo Parpola, *Letters from Assyrian Scholars to the Kings Esarhaddon and Assurbanipal, Part I: Texts* (AOAT 5/1; Kevelaer, Germany: Butzon & Bercker; Neukirchen-Vluyn: Neukirchener, 1970), 271–72, and *Part II: Commentary and Appendices* (AOAT 5/2; Kevelaer, Germany: Butzon & Bercker; Neukirchen-Vluyn: Neukirchener, 1983), 329, and Nissinen, *References*, 78–81.

30 SAA 10 352; see also Parpola, *Letters from Assyrian Scholars, I–II*, no. 280.

31 Maximilian Streck, *Assurbanipal und die letzten assyrischen Könige bis zum Untergange Niniveh's* (VAB 7; Leipzig: Hinrichs, 1916), 2:114–19, 188–95 (esp. B v 49–76); Rykle Borger, *Beiträge zum Inschriftenwerk Assurbanipals* (Wiesbaden: Harrassowitz, 1996), 101–3, 224–25. Note also another dream revelation without any direct speech (Parpola, *Assyrian Prophecies*, civ, n. 235, regarding *ABL* 1249 = SAA 13 139).

tion, the focus of the prophecies is reassurance to the king or royal family (queen mother), at times, as with the symbolic covenant, in dramatic fashion. Departing from the usual assurance to the king—apart from some complaints of neglect by Ištar, as already mentioned—is the letter in which an unidentified woman, speaking on behalf of a deity, tells a royal representative to "say in the king's presence" that certain items, given to others, should be returned to the deity who would then show beneficence to the king.[32] There are also rare references to prophets in connection with ordinary people. An aged scribe, having fallen from favor, pleading poverty and the lack of transportation, despairing of assistance from the king, appealed to a *raggimu* to no avail—"he lacked a vision" (*diglu*). So the old scribe turned again to the king—perhaps intrigued by being seen as more effective than a *raggimu*.[33]

In contrast to the Mari situation, in which steps are frequently taken to check a message's authenticity, the Neo-Assyrian prophecies have little indication of verification. Verification may have been reserved for dangerous or unfavorable prophecies. For example, a letter reports a divine word from the god Nusku through a slave girl belonging to Bel-ahu-uṣur, a word endorsing a conspirator as king—this endorsement, of course, is disquieting. The king is advised to summon the girl and to perform a ritual, probably an extispicy. The slave owner is to be summoned, together with others connected with the suspected conspirator; they shall all perish, it is predicted. The king is to check on others who might have told of the conspiracy but, contrary to their duty to inform, did not.[34] In related letters from the same sender, the follow-up advice is that possible conspirators should be put to death; the advice is presented as a word from Mullissu—"this word, it is from Mullissu"—thus suggesting that Mullissu, commonly cited for her concern for the king's well-being, overrules Nusku.[35] The writer insists that he is only carrying out his duty to the king, as one bound by oath to report any disquieting news. The focus seems to be on the possibility of conspiracy—whoever was involved, in whatever role—rather than on the confirmation of a seemingly divine word or a controversy

---

32 SAA 13 144.
33 SAA 10 294; Nissinen, *References*, 84–88.
34 Nissinen, *References*, 108–11.
35 *CT* 53 17:8–9; Nissinen, *References*, 111–15.

among the gods. The possibility that Nusku is speaking truly is apparently set aside, because the gods do not oppose the king.[36]

A similar reference to possible negative messages from the prophets appears in the treaty undertaken by Esarhaddon to assure Assurbanipal as his successor. The "duty to inform" is applied to a long list of sources with potentially bad news. These sources include friend or foe, the king's enemies and allies, the royal family, the families of the vassals, anything "not good, not pleasant, not proper . . . from the mouth of a *raggimu*-prophet, a *mahhû*-ecstatic, an inquirer of a divine word (*šāʾili amat ili*), or from anyone at all."[37] The issue is not so much whether the prophecy is "true" or "false," whether from a deity or not—the process apparently ignores the possibility that an unfavorable word could be from a deity—but whether the word is inimicable to the king. The king's self-interest determines truth or falsehood, which is not an uncommon position for a political leader.[38]

Little information is presented regarding the inspiration of the prophets. However, given the association or equation in the royal inscriptions of the *raggimu* with the *mahhû*—even though *mahhû*s are never identified explicitly with individual prophetic messages in Neo-Assyrian texts, but appear only as a summary category—inspiration was presumably by means of ecstasy, the "madness" of the *mahhû*. Dreams are cited only for others, such as the *šabrû*.

In the Neo-Assyrian texts, prophecy has a higher status than reflected in the Mari texts. The prophetic words, focusing on reassurance, were gathered into official collections that report only the words

---

36 What is most likely involved, as Nissinen notes, is an apparent controversy between the North Syrian center of Harran and the Assyrian heartland (ibid., 121–24). Nonetheless, performing an extispicy ritual on the slave-girl speaker—if that was to happen—would provide the only Neo-Assyrian example of "'checking' the accuracy of a prophecy by means of another divinatory method" (125). Ultimately, the conspiracy may have been part of an elaborate plot and counterplot, with the supposed successor actually a double agent of the king (150–53).

37 SAA 2 6:108–22.

38 Nissinen ("Falsche Prophetie in neuassyrischer und deuteronomistischer Darstellung," in *Das Deuteronimium und seine Querbeziehungen* [ed. T. Veijola; Schriften der Finnischen Exegetischen Gesellschaft 62; Helsinki: Finnische Exegetische Gesellschaft; Göttingen: Vandenhoeck & Ruprecht, 1996], 177) seems to cast the issue as true or untrue—"jeden Ausdruck der Untreue"—but allows that "true prophecy cannot, in any instance, be directed against the king or his crown prince" (180); see his discussion (193–95) concluding that there is no successful test regarding true or false prophecy, only the perspective of the party asking that question.

themselves, which seem to have taken on significance apart from their context, with but brief identifications of the speakers. But prophecy again, as indicated, *inter alia*, by the paucity of textual evidence compared to other forms of divine communication, is not the communication with highest status. The prophetic activity is associated particularly with the psychically active cult of Ištar of Arbela and her close associates, and points primarily to individual revelations.

Israel

Turning more briefly to prophecy in ancient Israel, on which there has been intensive study for a considerable time, we face a number of differences.[39] Whatever the at times somewhat grandiose claims, Israel is in reality a small-scale society, not a major international power like the kingdom of Mari or the Neo-Assyrian Empire. Apart from a few inscriptions, principally one of the Lachish letters, we have no contemporary documents or virtually contemporary collections of prophetic texts.[40] Instead of the brief periods reflected by the other two corpuses, with little obvious redaction, the biblical corpus reflects a long tradition of prophecy, preserved with considerable redaction. Rather than presenting "snapshots" in time, the biblical tradition is a many-layered portrait that has been considerably retouched. Additionally, a high percentage of the prophets—and not only the 450 and 400, respectively, cited in 1 Kgs 18—mentioned in the biblical tradition are prophets of Baal or Asherah.[41] The canonical or "classical" prophets, even purported prophets of Yahweh, regarded themselves outnumbered by prophets who did not have access to God's true intentions (1 Kgs 22). There were direct conflicts among the prophets. Israel also understood its foundational figures, specifically Moses, but also Samuel, to have been religious generalists best summarized by the

---

[39] For a recent survey of prophecy in Israel, see Joseph Blenkinsopp, *A History of Prophecy in Israel* (revised and enlarged edition; Louisville: Westminster John Knox Press, 1996).

[40] On the Lachish reference, see Simon B. Parker, "The Lachich Letters and Official Reactions to Prophecies," in *Uncovering Ancient Stones: Essays in Memory of H. Neil Richardson* (ed. L. M. Hopfe; Winona Lake, Ind.: Eisenbrauns, 1994), 65–78.

[41] There may have been considerable overlap between the prophets of Asherah and the prophets of Baal, given the ancient Near Eastern practice of individual affiliation with the cult of more than one deity.

terms *nābîʾ* or *ʾîš ʾelōhîm*. Israel honored prophecy, and many prophets had a powerful influence beyond their own historical moment.

Furthermore, from an early period Israel had an exclusivist group for whom religious legitimacy could only be connected with Yahweh. As such, Israel had to deal with the issue of true and false prophecy in a different way than its neighbors.

Individuals and Groups

In sheer numbers, the biblical references are unlike what we know from Mari or Assyria: 450 prophets of Baal (1 Kgs 18:22); four hundred of Asherah (1 Kgs 18:19); four hundred prophets of Yahweh under the leadership of Zedekiah ben Kenaanah (1 Kgs 22:6); one hundred prophets concealed in caves by Ahab's chief domestic official, Obadiah (1 Kgs 18:13); one hundred members of a prophetic band (*bĕnê han-nĕbîʾîm*) miraculously fed by Elisha (2 Kgs 4:43); seventy elders for whom Yahweh subdivided the spirit given to Moses, such that they "prophesied" (i.e., became ecstatic), if but once (Num 11:25); and the fifty-strong group that searched for Elijah (2 Kgs 2). But the vast majority of these "prophets" were really ecstatics, not prophets in the sense of conveying divine messages. It is the same for the prophetic groups (*ḥebel nĕbîʾîm* or *lahăqat han-nĕbîʾîm*) in the time of Samuel (1 Sam 10:5, 10; 19:20). These groups focused on the cult of ecstasy, without parallel in the Mari or Neo-Assyrian texts, which report only individual ecstasy, although there are some indications of group ecstasy in other texts.[42] Plural forms for the *āpilum* and *muhhûm* occur in the Mari texts, as noted, and there are references to *raggimānu* and *raggimātu* (plurals) in Assyrian texts. But the only indication of group activity by the Mari or Assyrian prophets is the Mari reference to *nabû*s (ARM 26 216), who apparently offer a collective response to inquiry in a way parallel to 1 Kgs 22.

Many of the Israelite prophets must have been cultic or at least court personnel, although, given the fluidity of roles, it is difficult to identify individual prophets in this regard. Gad is identified as *han-nābîʾ ḥōzê dāwīd* (2 Sam 24:11), as *ḥōzê dāwīd* (1 Chr 21:9), and as *ḥōzê ham-melek* (2 Chr 29:25); Jahaziel, a well-credentialed Levite of the

---

42 The most striking reference appears in a Middle Babylonian text from Ugarit (*Ugaritica* 5 162.11), which says that "my brothers, like ecstatics (*mahhû*s), are bathed/drenched in their own blood."

Asaph clan, is overwhelmed by the spirit of God during the royal petition for aid in war, and offers a divine oracle of assurance to the king and the people (2 Chr 20). The offer is similar to some of the Mari prophetic texts, but that does not mean that Jahaziel was institutionally programmed. The prophets who proclaimed what the king or the people wanted to hear—at least from the perspective of the present biblical text—might be suspect, but that does not in itself qualify them as regularized cultic prophets.

The titles for Israel's prophets offer little continuity with the Mari and Assyrian titles, but those titles are, for the most part, transparent in the local language. In the Israelite tradition, the titles occur occasionally in self-reference, but typically, like the Near Eastern titles, are supplied by others. The most common Israelite title, *nābîʾ*, which functionally means "an ecstatic who might also prophesy"—the somewhat elusive etymology is not as relevant as the usage—now has its linguistic parallel in the one Mari text, and *nabû* is also known as a title from Late Bronze Emar, together with the related *munabbiʾātu*. But there is no secure information about the function of these persons at Emar—they may be "singers."[43] Only the title *nābîʾ* identifies the groups of prophets reported in the Bible, although the leader of such a group may also be called by the second-most frequent title, *ʾîš (hā-)ʾelohîm*, the simple "man of (the) god." This title is also used of David a few times and has a possible Near Eastern parallel.[44] The third title, *ḥōzê*, "visionary," is used of Gad, Iddo, Jehu, and Amos—never as a self-reference—and again has its parallel outside the Mari-Assyria traditions, specifically in North Syria (Zakkur inscription, ca. 800 B.C.E., as a plural) and in the Balaam tradition of ninth-century Transjordan.[45]

---

43 See Daniel Fleming, "The Etymological Origins of the Hebrew *nābîʾ*: The One Who Invokes God," *CBQ* 55 (1993): 217–24.

44 For a possible Hittite parallel in the Plague Prayers of Mursilis, (*antuhša-*) *šiuniyant-*, "homme habite du dieu," see René Lebrun, *Hymnes et prieres hittites* (Homo Religiosus 4; Louvain-la-neuve: Centre d'histoire des religions, 1980), 37, 175, and esp. 215; E. Laroche, "Les noms anatoliens du 'dieu' et leurs derives," *JCS* 21 (1967): 176.

45 For the Zakkur inscription, see *TSSI* 2, no. 5:12 (pl.); for Balaam as a "visionary of the gods," see Jo Ann Hackett, *The Balaam Text from Deir ʿAlla* (Chico, Calif.: Scholars Press, 1984), 25.

Gender

Unlike Mari and Assyria, the prophets in Israel are predominantly male, unless the plurals with reference to the large prophetic groups conceal some females. The only women with the title *nĕbîʾâ* are Miriam, the singer; Deborah, the singer, war leader, and judge; the woman who presumably was so titled as Isaiah's wife; Huldah, the well-known contemporary of King Josiah; and Noadiah, the prophetic opponent of Nehemiah. There are also the women who prophesy "from their (own) hearts" (*mitmabbĕʾôt*) in Ezek 13:17, but with their attributed functions they are more likely being described as ecstatics, although their specific role is difficult to sort out from the polemics.[46] Of these women, only Huldah is specifically associated with a prophecy, and Noadiah (MT) is, perhaps slanderously, viewed as false because of her opposition to Nehemiah. Yet the high-status Mari *āpilum/āpiltum*, with only two females out of sixteen or more—unlike the more balanced *muhhûm/muhhūtum* and the rather evenly distributed prophets without titles—may offer a clue to the gender distribution in Israel. The society may have viewed the role as properly masculine in spite of its more egalitarian charismatic origination. In spite of many similarities, it is clear that prophecy played a more prominent role in Israel than in the Mari society.[47]

Standing

Whatever Israelite prophets' popularity in their own lifetime, they clearly were of immense and lasting importance. Apart from their models among the foundational figures, the prophets were involved in the anointing and discarding—public or private—of kings. (Granted, at times they apparently thought they were endorsing a *nāgîd* rather than a *melek*.) A prophet even declared that a foreign king, Cyrus, was the coming "anointed one." In this role they have a forerunner in what the *āpilum* of Addu, from northeast Syria, declared about the king of Mari. The standing of the prophet is exemplified by the encounter, perhaps legendary, but nonetheless revealing, between the powerful King Ahab of Israel and the prophet Elijah: Ahab tells Elijah that he is

[46] On this text, see now Nancy R. Bowen, "The Daughters of Your People: Female Prophets in Ezekiel 13:17–23," *JBL* 118 (1999): 417–33.

[47] Note Simon B. Parker, "Official Attitudes toward Prophecy at Mari and in Israel," *VT* 43 (1993): 50–68, esp. 67–68.

"the one who troubles Israel," and Elijah responds, "I have not troubled Israel, but you and your father's house have" (1 Kgs 8:17–18). The prophets often address the king directly, and their words otherwise are easily conveyed. In most of these encounters that annoyed the king, the prophet nonetheless survived. The member of the prophetic band who carried out Elisha's orders and anointed Jehu may have been dismissed by Jehu as a *mĕšuggaʿ*, "a crazy man," but Jehu was ready to act on what the "crazy man" did (2 Kgs 9:1–13). The prophets are often consulted, even though the king—just like the people—may reject the message.

The prophets—as with the symbolic treaty described by the *raggimu* of Ištar of Arbela—could also serve as covenant mediators. Samuel is a prime example. They may also announce a new covenant—for example, Hosea and Jeremiah—and they frequently take initiative as innovators, as illustrated by Hosea, Second Isaiah, and others. The prophets are both advocates of established traditions and harbingers of new possibilities. The Israelite prophets, individually and cumulatively, played a more important role in Israel than their counterparts in Mari or Assyria.

The message of the prophets is both judgment and salvation—rarely one without the other. They express God's ultimate commitment to Israel and insist that, whatever the present, Israel will have a splendorous future. They also place themselves within the community, whatever its future. As with the *muhhûm* in the Mari text who dramatically ate raw lamb, the Israelite prophets often reinforced their message with strange symbolic acts.

A primary addressee is the king, but the focus is not the king's personal safety and well-being—on how to keep the king safely in power or to improve the king's attention to cultic acts—but on the king's behavior as it connected with the overall worship of Yahweh and the maintenance of justice and righteousness in the king's realm.

The Charge of Falsehood

One consequence of the exclusivist tradition prevalent among certain groups in Israel, and of the prophetic penchant for thinking and acting independently of the reigning monarch, is conflict between the kings and the prophets and conflict among the prophets themselves. Unlike Mari and Assyria, in which different cult centers might have had different agendas and might have offered conflicting or unsought advice, but in which no one charged deliberate falsehood, Israelite prophets were willing to charge each other with being deceptive or false.

Intriguingly, the accuser does not always say that the false prophet is aware of falsehood or that the prophets are making something up (see Ezek 13:2–4). In the revealing story in 1 Kgs 22, Micaiah says that he overheard the deliberation in Yahweh's council that led to the recommendation, approved by God, "I will go and be a lying spirit in the mouths of all [the king's] prophets" (v. 22). According to Micaiah, the king's prophets were being duped in recommending battle. Ezekiel 14:9–10 affirms that prophets who speak deceptively may have been intentionally deceived by God. In response to Micaiah's charge of a lying spirit, Zedekiah ben Kenaʿanah, the leader of the four hundred, immediately disputes this allegation and defends his authenticity. The king's response was to do what he wanted, albeit with precautions, and to clap Micaiah into jail. This was bad news for Micaiah, but he—or the redactor—appealed to another criterion of falsehood: "If you (O king) ever do get home safely, Yahweh has not spoken through me." But, whatever happened, Micaiah was in serious trouble. In another story (2 Kgs 8), Elisha openly offers a two-pronged oracle to Hazael of Damascus: (*a*) King Ben-Hadad is going to die, but tell him he will recover; (*b*) Hazael will become king in place of Ben-Hadad. Hazael follows Elisha's advice but decides to help the prediction by suffocating Ben-Hadad.

Micaiah's appeal to historical outcome as a means of verification, a criterion used by others as well, especially the Deuteronomistic tradition, does not help people make decisions at the moment. The appeal also lacks clarity, as for many of the widely heralded prophecies that have not come true, such as the announcement of the peaceful kingdom. Even when known, these outcomes are ambiguous. In Jer 37:18–19, Jeremiah complains to the king that, unlike the unpunished prophets who said that the Babylonians would not attack Israel, Jeremiah, despite historical vindication, does not get respect. Another example is the interplay between Jeremiah and those baking raisin cakes for the Queen of Heaven. Although bakers ceased their practice, presumably at least in part at Jeremiah's urging (Jer 7:16–20), the fall of Jerusalem was not adverted. The devotees of the queen took this as a sign of the goddess's anger rather than of insufficient repentance toward Yahweh, and resumed their baking (Jer 44:24–28).

In the dispute between Jeremiah and Hananiah, the suggestion is that truth is on the side of those who prophesy disaster. This standard has difficulties, not only for prophets of salvation such as Second Isaiah, but also for those who judge what constitutes a disaster. Note, however, that Hananiah not only predicts an early return from Babylon of the temple furnishings, which presumably would please most Judeans, he also predicts—according to the text—the return of King Jehoiachin (Jer 28:4), which, considering the Judean power structures, would not have been good news for Jehoiachin's uncle, King Zedekiah, and somewhat risky for Hananiah.[48] Also acceptable as an accusation but not susceptible to verification is the charge that false prophets proclaim their personal dreams as revelatory, rather than having been given access to the deliberations of God's council (Jer 23).

Ideology played a primary role in judging falsehood. If the prophecy was displeasing to the king or the people, or whoever was arbiter, it was likely to be discarded out of hand. Deuteronomy 13 advises that a prophet or a dreamer who offers signs or wonders, who uses the accomplished signs or wonders to encourage people to follow another god, is being used by God to test the people. Such a misleading prophet, even if being used by God, should be put to death. More restrictive is the intimation in Deut 18:14–20 that the coming prophet—or any prophet—must be from within the community and must be like Moses; that is, no future prophet could disagree with Moses and be genuine. In short, there was no real means of empirical verification.

Inspiration

The prophets report theophanies, visions, auditions, and dreams, while having their own vehicles of choice for revelation. Ecstasy underlies much of Israelite prophecy, although there must have been those adept at quickly putting themselves into an ecstatic or "altered state of consciousness."

48 Robert P. Carroll notes that Hananiah "is in defiance of Zedekiah, the court and the Babylonians," a formidable list of opponents (*Jeremiah* [OTL; Philadelphia: Westminster Press, 1986], 543). Hananiah is not just playing to the crowd.

Conclusion

Among prophets in Mari, Assyria, and Israel, we find many variations and "exaggerations" of the possibilities of prophetic revelation. There are many possibilities, and each community is distinctive. Prophecy was a living phenomenon, and each community, for unknown reasons, selected different options from the prophetic alternatives. The three corpuses are valuable because of the range of activity they report. As such, it is easier to see commonalities and anomalies among prophets, and to appreciate different ways in which prophetic revelation played a role in societies of the ancient Near East.[49]

[49] I am preparing a booklength treatment of prophecy in the ancient Near East, which will expand and, hopefully, clarify points here. For Mari, the masterful studies by J.-M. Durand, D. Charpin, and Jack M. Sasson offer a wealth of insight and information, and Abraham Malamat has been a keen observer of the mutual illumination of prophecy in the Mari texts and in Israel (see especially his *Mari and the Early Israelite Experience* [Schweich Lectures, 1984; Oxford: Oxford University Press, 1989], 70–121, and his *Mari and the Bible* [SHANE 12; Leiden: Brill, 1998]). For the Neo-Assyrian texts, the cited studies by Parpola and Nissinen have special importance; see also Martti Nissinen, "Die Relevanz der neuassyrischen Prophetie für die alttestamentliche Forschung," in *Mesopotamica—Ugaritica—Biblica: Festschrift für Kurt Bergerhof* (ed. M. Dietrich and O. Loretz; AOAT 232; Kevelaer, Germany: Butzon & Bercker; Neukirchen-Vluyn: Neukirchener, 1993), 217–58.

5

Mesopotamian Prophecy between Immanence and Transcendence: A Comparison of Old Babylonian and Neo-Assyrian Prophecy

Karel van der Toorn

Introduction

Over the past century, many genres of the Hebrew Bible have been fruitfully compared with relevant literature from neighboring civilizations of the ancient Near East. Biblical laws, rituals, historiography, prayers, and wisdom have counterparts in the literature of the Mesopotamians, Hittites, Canaanites, and Egyptians. Prophecy, however, was long considered a uniquely biblical phenomenon. Since the publication of a considerable number of ancient Mesopotamian prophecies, this view can no longer be upheld. Biblical scholars who realize this fact have devoted their efforts to studies of the relationship between biblical and Mesopotamian prophecy. Such is not the aim of this contribution. I limit myself to an investigation of Mesopotamian prophecy in order to demonstrate the internal differences and developments of what is often treated as a monolithic phenomenon. While not entering into a comparison with the Bible, I am convinced that the conclusions of this study will be relevant to students of Hebrew prophecy as well.

The evidence for ancient Mesopotamian prophecy is limited to Old Babylonian and Neo-Assyrian texts. The vast majority of the Old Babylonian texts come from the archives of Mari; they are conveniently accessible in an edition by Jean-Marie Durand.[1] The Neo-Assyrian texts

[1] Jean-Marie Durand, *Archives Epistolaires de Mari* I/1 (ARM 26; Paris: Editions Recherche sur les Civilisations, 1988), 377–452. For other relevant texts, see Bertrand Lafont, "Le roi de Mari et les prophètes du dieu Adad," *RA* 78 (1984): 7–18 (A. 1121 + A. 2731); Maria deJong Ellis, "The Goddess Kititum Speaks to King

come from the Assurbanipal library in Nineveh; they have been recently collected and translated by Simo Parpola.[2]

Neo-Assyrian prophecy is a thousand years younger than its Old Babylonian counterpart. If only for that reason, then, methodological rigor requires us to treat the two bodies of evidence separately; they should not be put in one box as though they reflect the same phenomenon. Yet once the distinct nature of Old Babylonian and Neo-Assyrian prophecy is recognized, there is also something to be learned from a comparison between them. Such comparisons have been made before, usually with a focus on their similarities (the ecstatic nature of prophecy, its role as a means of royal propaganda, and the like).[3] The comparison I make in the present contribution, however, is a comparison of contrast.

In what follows I discuss four points of contrast. They concern (1) the purpose of the written record of prophetic oracles, (2) the perception of the person of the prophet or prophetess, (3) the cultic context of prophecy, and (4) the way in which the prophecies depict the intervention of the gods.

The four contrasts do not stand in isolation from one another. They reflect a set of changes in the conception of the gods and their communication with human beings. Should one wish to capture these changes in one term, the word "transcendence" springs to mind. In the Neo-Assyrian conception, the gods belong to a different world, far removed from the mundane realities of our world. Contact with these gods was channeled through specialized intermediaries whose revelations were credited with enduring significance.

Ibalpiel: Oracle Texts from Ishchali," *MARI* 5 (1987): 235–66 (FLP 1674 and FLP 2064); Jean-Marie Durand, "Le mythologème du combat entre le dieu de l'orage et la mer en Mésopotamie," *MARI* 7 (1993): 41–61, esp. 43–45 (A. 1968); ARM 26 233; 238; 371.

2 Simo Parpola, *Assyrian Prophecies* (SAA 9; Helsinki: Helsinki University Press, 1997). See also SAA 13 139. For reports on prophecy see Martti Nissinen, *References to Prophecy in Neo-Assyrian Sources* (SAAS 7; Helsinki: Neo-Assyrian Text Corpus Project, 1998).

3 See, e.g., Manfried Dietrich, "Prohetie in den Keilschrifttexten," *Jahrbuch für Anthropologie und Religionsgeschichte* 1 (1973): 15–44; Karel van der Toorn, "L'oracle de victoire comme expression prophétique au Proche-Orient ancien," *RB* 94 (1987): 63–97; Herbert B. Huffmon, "Ancient Near Eastern Prophecy," *ABD* 5:477–82.

Prophecy in Writing

In a study dealing with the so-called "prophetic letters" from Old Babylonian Mari, I noted that the Babylonian prophets were primarily speakers, whose oracles were meant for a one-time oral performance. Although we only know about these prophecies by written reports, writing was not used as a means of preservation, but as an aid in the communication of the prophetic message on a synchronic level, that is, to contemporaries of the prophets.[4] No attempt was made by the Old Babylonian scribes to collect prophetic utterances for later generations. Once the events addressed by a prophet had come to pass, the prophecy had served its purpose. Prophecies were punctual, relevant only in connection with single historical events. Beyond those events, prophecies lost their value.

The situation of the Neo-Assyrian prophecies is strikingly different. The majority of the known Neo-Assyrian prophecies have been preserved in oracle collections (SAA 9 nos. 1–4).[5] In these collections we find the text of about twenty prophecies, each followed by the name of the prophet or prophetess (*ša pî*) and his or her city of provenance. Although the historical circumstances can often be tentatively reconstructed, there is no explicit reference to them in the texts or their subscriptions. The same holds true for the spot where the prophecy was delivered. It should be noted, in this connection, that the town or city from which the prophets come need not coincide with the place where they spoke their prophecy. There are several cases in which the two clearly differ. A woman from Dara-ahuya, a town in the mountains, delivered her prophecy, to judge by its contents, in Arbela (SAA 9 1.3); Tašmetu-ereš, a prophet of unknown provenance, prophesied in the city of Arbela as well (SAA 9 6); and the woman Dunnaša-amur (or Sinqiša-amur) from Arbela spoke a prophecy in Nineveh (SAA 9 9).[6]

The Neo-Assyrian collection tablets are relatively large, vertical tablets with two or three columns. This type, known as *ṭuppu*, was used for treaties, census lists, inventories, as well as for collections of all sorts, including royal decrees and the like. They were specifically

---

4 Karel van der Toorn, "Old Babylonian Prophecy between the Oral and the Written," *JNSL* 24 (1998): 55–70, esp. 69.

5 Parpola, *Assyrian Prophecies.*

6 On Dunnaša-amur and her possible identity with Sinqiša-amur, see ibid., il–l. For the historical and geographical context of the prophecy, see ibid., lxxi.

drawn up for archival storage and reference purposes. There is evidence that information recorded on these collection tablets was copied from smaller *u'iltu* tablets containing individual prophetic reports. Once these had been copied, they were routinely destroyed. Indeed, there is virtually no overlap between the prophecies in the collection tablets and those known from oracle reports on *u'iltu* tablets.[7] Three out of the four oracle collections presently at our disposal were all compiled by the same scribe, in contradistinction to the reports (*u'iltus*) written by different scribes.[8] These facts point to a deliberate policy on the part of the royal bureaucracy to preserve at least a fair number of the individual prophecies for later use.

The collection tablets, then, dissociate the individual prophecies from their immediate historical contexts. To what use were they put? A minimalist answer to this question would see the collection tablets as archival documents that were kept as records. Such a solution is unattractive because there is no information on chronology or historical circumstances. A maximalist answer to our question—what is the purpose of the collection tablets?—would see them as documents containing revelations relevant beyond their original context. The lack of historical information points toward this solution. These prophecies were not exhausted, so to speak, by their first fulfillment. They remained relevant, also with respect to new circumstances.

The plausibility of the maximalist view increases as one investigates the incentive for the compilation of the collections. A good illustration is Oracle Collection One (I follow the numbering adopted by Simo Parpola in SAA 9). Its ten prophecies refer to the events surrounding the accession of Esarhaddon in 681, as a study of the various motifs—battle, the crossing of the river, exile of the crown prince while his half-brothers are in power, triumphal celebration, and so on—indicates. Thematically there is a striking resemblance to Nineveh Inscription A, in which Esarhaddon describes his accession to the throne, his overcoming all difficulties, and the constant encouragement he received from the gods by means of prophets.[9] Nineveh In-

---

[7] See ibid., liii.

[8] See ibid., lv–lvi.

[9] See Rykle Borger, *Die Inschriften Asarhaddons Königs von Assyrien* (AfOB 9; Graz, Austria: Selbstverlag, 1956; repr., Osnabrück, Germany: Biblio-Verlag, 1967), 40–45. For a study of the references to prophets in this text, see Nissinen, *References*, 30–34.

scription A was written at the beginning of 673. This was the time Esarhaddon designated Assurbanipal as his successor. The purpose of the inscription, written almost ten years after the reported events, was to remind potential critics and pretenders to the throne of the support the heir designate would enjoy. Just as the gods had stood by Esarhaddon, so they would stand by Assurbanipal. A similar motivation may be supposed to lie behind the compilation of the first oracle collection. The oracles of encouragement which Esarhaddon once received were still valid for his son.

If this tentative reconstruction of the genesis and purpose of Oracle Collection One has merit—and let me acknowledge my debt to Simo Parpola for the reconstruction[10]—the Neo-Assyrian oracle collections would not attest to the mere preservation, but to the recycling of prophecy. The assumption underlying this procedure implies that divine words once spoken do not lose their validity after a first fulfillment.[11] The prophetic oracles lend themselves to a second life by virtue of a dual characteristic: they are formulated in general terms (thus they typically refer to "your enemy" rather than to named adversaries), and they are set within a royal ideology focusing on the king as a representative of a dynasty.[12] Promises of support for one member of that dynasty hold good for his legitimate heir as well.

The dynastic perspective of the Neo-Assyrian prophecies becomes very explicit in the following quotation:

> You shall be safe in your palace. Your son and your grandson shall rule as kings on the lap of Ninurta.[13]

We may draw a parallel with the dynastic prophecy concerning the house of David in 2 Sam 7:12, which served to legitimate David's successors as well:

---

10 Parpola, *Assyrian Prophecies*, lxviii–lxix.

11 So, too, Nissinen, *References*, 172 ("the prophecies were no longer disposable *ad hoc* utterances concerning a special case but became part of the written tradition, a reference record that could be used and interpreted by succeeding generations").

12 Note the prominence of the theme of the birth and early youth of the king (e.g. SAA 9 1.4 ii 20'–26'); the insistence on his being the *aplu kēnu*, "rightful heir" (SAA 9 1.6 iv 5–6, 20); and the "everlasting" establishment of the throne (SAA 9 1.6 iii 19'–22').

13 SAA 9 1.10 vi 25–30; cf. 2.3 ii 13'–14'.

> When your days are fulfilled and you lie down with your fathers, I will raise up your offspring after you, who shall come forth from your body, and I will establish his kingdom.

Although the dynastic outlook is not entirely lacking in the Old Babylonian prophecies, its scope is merely retrospective.[14] The long-term vision inherent to the dynastic outlook of the Neo-Assyrian oracles is consonant with the recycling of prophecy, even if it does not constitute by itself a compelling reason for recycling.

Concomitant with the Neo-Assyrian effort to collect certain prophecies and to preserve them for posterity are references to earlier prophecies as authoritative texts. We find such references both in the prophecies themselves and in letters of counsel to the king. Manfred Weippert has studied the phenomenon of prophecy quoted in prophecy.[15] His most telling example is a prophecy by Mulissu-kabtat, speaking in the name of Mulissu, addressing King Assurbanipal.[16] The first half of the prophecy consists of a more or less literal reminder of a prophecy Assurbanipal received when still crown prince. This prophecy has now come true and should infuse the king with confidence in the second prophecy, introduced by the phrase, "And now Mulissu says . . ."[17] Quotation of an earlier prophecy in correspondence addressed to the king is found in a letter by Nabû-nadin-šumi to Esarhaddon. He quotes a line from an oracle by Ištar of Nineveh and Ištar of Arbela, saying: "We shall root out from Assyria those who are not loyal to the king, our lord." This prophetic utterance is put forth in support of measures of banishment against a troublemaker whose identity we cannot establish.[18]

Both the prophecy collections and the prophetic quotations are significant as novel understandings of prophecy—novel, that is, by com-

---

14 Thus Addu is said to have returned Zimri-Lim to the throne of his father; see Lafont, "Roi de Mari et les prophètes," 7–18, esp. 11, 16–18, 51; A. 1968 r. 1'–2' (*MARI* 7 [1993]: 43–45). Cf. ARM 26 217:21–23: "[What] I gave of old in the hand [of your fathers] I [now] will gi[ve] to you."

15 Manfred Weippert, "'Das Frühere, siehe, ist eingetroffen . . .': Über Selbstzitate im altorientalischen Prophetenspruch," in *Oracles et prophéties dans l'antiquité: Actes du Colloque de Strasbourg, 15–17 Juin 1995* (ed. Jean-Georges Heintz; Université des Sciences Humaines de Strasbourg, Travaux du Centre de Recherche sur le Proche-Orient et la Grèce antiques 15; Paris: De Boccard, 1997), 147–69.

16 SAA 9 7. The text is discussed in ibid., 153–57.

17 SAA 9 7:12. For the rendering of this line, see ibid., 156 and n. 32.

18 SAA 10 284, quotation rev. 6–8. For an extensive discussion see Nissinen, *References*, 102–5.

parison with the Old Babylonian prophecies. Prophecies are no longer ad hoc utterances, meaningful once but irrelevant ever after, but on the contrary are valid over a longer period of time. Prophecy is the word of God, and the word of God transcends the situation to which it originally applied. It has enduring significance. The same conception explains the use of prophecy in a ritual context, a prime example of which is the so-called Covenant of Aššur. The latter is a collection of prophecies to be recited at the (annual?) celebration of Esarhaddon's kingship.[19] Neo-Assyrian prophecy thus foreshadows what may be termed the "frozen" prophecy in the Babylonian liturgy of the New Year Festival as it had been preserved in Hellenistic Uruk. Introduced by the characteristic phrase *lā tapallah* ("fear not!"), the priest assures the king that Bel will bless him forever, destroy his enemies, and overthrow his adversaries.[20]

Neo-Assyrian prophecy, then, is closer to biblical prophecy than the Old Babylonian prophecies, not only in time but also with respect to the underlying view of prophecy as the word of God with enduring value, applicable to more than one situation. Whereas Old Babylonian prophecy is punctual, so to speak, Neo-Assyrian prophecy is durative, transcending the historical circumstances which prompted its first deliverance.

The Person of the Prophet

A second point in which Neo-Assyrian prophecy differs from Old Babylonian prophecy—and in which, incidentally, it resembles biblical prophecy—pertains to the person of the prophet.

The Neo-Assyrian prophets whose prophecies have been preserved on collection tablets or oracle reports are accredited prophets; accredited, that is, by the royal bureaucracy, on the strength of the contents of their predictions. They are never anonymous. Their name and city of provenance are recorded alongside their prophecies. Some of

---

19 SAA 9 3. Parpola suggests that Collection Three "is likely to have been recited at the coronation of Esarhaddon" (*Assyrian Prophecies*, lxx; cf. lxiv) and points out the connection with the *tākultu*-ritual (22). On the possibility of an annual renewal of the Assyrian kingship, see A. Kirk Grayson, "The Early Development of Assyrian Monarchy," *UF* 3 (1971): 318–19 and n. 50; Richard I. Caplice and Wolfgang Heimpel, "Investitur," *RlA* 5:139–44, esp. 141.

20 François Thureau-Dangin, *Rituels Accadiens* (1921; repr., Osnabrück, Germany: Zeller, 1975), 144–45, nos. 434–46.

these names turn up more than once in the documents at our disposal. Thus the prophet La-dagil-ili from Arbela is mentioned as the author (or medium, if one prefers) of six different prophecies.[21] Sinqiša-amur (Dunnaša-amur) and Bayâ are likewise prophets with more than one "official" prophecy to their name.[22] The authority of the prophecy assumes the authority of the prophet in question.

The Old Babylonian prophets, preceding their Neo-Assyrian counterparts by more than a millennium, found themselves in a different situation. Their individual identity (personal name and city of provenance) was of little concern to their contemporaries. We do know the names of some of the Mari prophets, but these have not been recorded because the identity of the prophet conferred authority on his message.[23] Old Babylonian prophecies were checked by means of extispicy. This so-called *piqittum* procedure was not meant to assess the authenticity of the prophetic experience, but to establish whether or not the prophet's message should be acted upon.[24] Although some token of the prophet's identity was needed to perform the *piqittum* (a fringe of clothing, a lock of hair), the identity of the prophet never by itself guaranteed the validity of his prophecy.

The Neo-Assyrian prophets differed from their Old Babylonian colleagues in yet another aspect. Whereas the Old Babylonian prophets might be connected to the cults of a variety of gods (Adad, Šamaš, Dagan, Marduk, Annunitum, Diritum, Belet-ekallim, Ninhursagga), the overwhelming majority of the Neo-Assyrian prophets are connected in one form or another with the cult of the goddess Ištar.[25] When gods other than Ištar, such as Bel or Nabû, address the king by means of prophecy, they use the channel of a prophet or prophetess

---

21 SAA 9 1.10; 2.3; 3.2–5.

22 SAA 9 1.2; 2.5; 9; 10 (Sinqiša-amur/Dunnaša-amur); SAA 9 1.4; 2.2 (Bayâ).

23 Among the Old Babylonian prophets identified by name, we find Iṣi-ahum, an *āpilum* active in the temple of Hišamītum (ARM 26 195); Šelebum, an *assinnum* of Annunitum (cf. n. 29); Lupahum, the *āpilum* of Dagan (ARM 26 199:5); Hubatum, a prophetess of Annunitum (ARM 26 200:5); the *āpiltum* Innibana (ARM 26 204:4); Qišti-Diritum, the *āpilum* of Diritum (ARM 26 208:5–6); Ili-haznaya, an *assinnum* of Annunitum (ARM 26 212); the lay prophetess Ahatum (ARM 26 214:6–7); one Irra-gamil (ARM 26 222:12); the ecstatics Hadnu-El and Iddin-Kubi (ARM 26 227); and Abiya, the *āpilum* of Addu of Aleppo (*MARI* 7 [1993]: 43, A. 1968:3). See also ARM 26 nos. 211; 221-bis.

24 See Durand, *Archives,* 409.

25 See Parpola, *Assyrian Prophecies,* xlvii–xlviii.

of Ištar.[26] Unlike Simo Parpola, I do not think this means that in these cases Ištar is "putting on new masks" to speak on behalf of other members of some sort of Holy Trinity.[27] Bel and Nabû can speak for themselves, but they do so through the agency of the Ištar prophets. The distinction might seem a subtle one, but it is not without importance. In Neo-Assyrian times, prophecy was a type of divination pertaining to the province of Ištar, as extispicy was a type of divination connected with the gods Šamaš and Adad.

Neo-Assyrian prophecy owes its privileged link to the cult of Ištar to the shamanistic nature which the two have in common. The Neo-Assyrian prophets are ecstatics. They "shout" (*ragāmu*) and "go into a frenzy" (*mahû*, N-stem). Such behavior fits well with the character of the cult of Ištar, which was strongly shamanistic. Ištar was deemed capable to produce, by way of ecstasy, a metamorphosis in her worshipers. Men might be turned into women, and women were made to behave as men. If ever there was a possession cult in Mesopotamia, it was connected to Ištar.[28] Prophecy, being a type of divination based on inspiration, is at home in such a cult. There is evidence that at least some of the Neo-Assyrian prophetesses were in reality men, or rather self-castrated transvestites.[29] Their outward appearance was interpreted as a display of Ištar's transforming powers. Possessed by the divine, they were the obvious persons to become mouthpieces of the gods.

The association between prophecy and the cult of Ištar (or one of her allomorphs) was not unknown in Old Babylonian times. A case in point is that of Šelebum, a transvestite (*assinnum*) belonging to the cult personnel of Annunitum, mentioned as the medium of prophetic oracles in three Mari letters.[30] What remained an occasional link in Mari, however, has become a structural connection in first-millennium Assyria. By then, prophets, as a rule, are named individuals whom Ištar has endowed with powers to act as a medium between gods and humankind. We may perhaps speak, in this connection, of a professionalization of prophecy.

---

26 See, e.g., SAA 9 1.4; SAA 13 139.

27 Parpola, *Assyrian Prophecies*, xviii.

28 Brigitte Groneberg, *Lob der Ištar: Gebet und Ritual an die altbabylonische Venusgöttin* (Cuneiform Monographs 8; Groningen, Netherlands: Styx, 1997), 152–54.

29 Such as Bayâ and Ilussa-amur; see Parpola, *Assyrian Prophecies*, il–l.

30 See ARM 26 197:4; 198; 213. Note also the reference to Ili-haznaya, another *assinnum* of Annunitum (ARM 26 212).

The Cultic Context of Prophecy

Mari: The Temple as the Theater of Prophecy

A third difference between Old Babylonian and Neo-Assyrian prophecy concerns its cultic context. The Old Babylonian gods grant prophetic revelations only in the sanctuary. Dreams may occur at other places, but prophecy, properly speaking, is confined to the temple. This is an important point that has not always received the attention it deserves.

The point can be illustrated with a few examples from the Mari archives. The royal servant who is to keep the king informed about the prophecies from Terqa, a famous religious center, hears the oracles as they happen "in the temple of the god."[31] When a god speaks directly through the mouth of a prophet, the latter utters the prophecy first in the temple. The prophet (*āpilum* or *āpiltum*) "rises" (*itbi*) or "stands" (*izziz*) to deliver the divine message in the temple.[32] The ecstatic (*muhhûm*), too, receives the revelation in a sanctuary; this is the place where he or she gets into a frenzy (*immahi, immahu*),[33] utters loud cries (*šitassû*),[34] and gives the oracle.[35] When a prophet delivers an oracle outside the sanctuary, at the residence of the royal deputy for instance, he repeats an oracle revealed to him in the sanctuary.[36] For that reason the prophet presents himself as a messenger of the god (DN, *išpuranni*):[37] he transmits the message (*ṭēmum*), which he received at an earlier stage.[38]

The notion of the temple as a place of revelation comes to the fore

---

31 ARM 26 196:8–10: *ig*[*e*]*rrûm ša ina bīt ilim i*[*ba*]*ššû u tešemmû a*[*n*]*a ṣēr*[*iy*]*a šupram.*

32 A. 1121 + 2731 (= *RA* 84 [1987]: 7–18): 29–30 (Addu temple at Aleppo); ARM 26 195:5–7 (temple of Hišamitum); 204:4–5 (Belet-ekallim temple); 209:4–7 (during sacrifices for Dagan); 211:5–9 (Belet-ekallim temple); 219:4'–6' (Ninhursagga temple).

33 ARM 26 213:4–7; 214:5–7.

34 ARM 26 202:15–6; cf. 7–8.

35 ARM 26 200:3–6 (Annunitum temple); 215:9–16 (Dagan temple at Tuttul); 227:6–20 (Abba temple, dream report); 237:22–3 (Annunitum temple).

36 ARM 26 212:5–12; cf. r. 10'–11', in which the *assinnum* (transvestite) of Annunitum comes to the palace and delivers an oracle received in the temple of Annunitum.

37 ARM 26 210:11 (a woman married to a free citizen, on behalf of Dagan); 220:19 (*muhhûm* of Dagan); 221:15 (*muhhûm* of Dagan).

38 ARM 26 212 r. 10'–11'; cf. no. 414:32–3.

in several dream reports as well. The dream of one Malik-Dagan offers a fine illustration.

> In my dream I was going, together with a companion, from the district of Saggaratum, through the upper district, to Mari. Before I got to my destination, I entered Terqa. As soon as I had come into Terqa I visited the temple of Dagan, and did obeisance to Dagan. As I did obeisance, Dagan opened his mouth and spoke to me in these terms: Have the Yaminite rulers and their armies made peace with Zimri-Lim's army that has come up? I said: They did not make peace. Just before I left he spoke to me: Why is it that Zimri-Lim's messengers are not steadily present before me? And why doesn't he put a complete report before me? Had he done so, I would have delivered the Yaminites into Zimri-Lim's hand a long time ago. Go now, I send you. You shall say to Zimri-Lim: Send me your messengers and put a complete report before me. Then I will make the Yaminites crawl in a fisherman's box and put them at your disposal.[39]

There is nothing in this account to suggest that Malik-Dagan was in the temple when he received the dream; this is not a case of incubation or temple sleep.[40] And yet his dream was clearly a revelation, culminating in his being commissioned to deliver a message to the king. Not only does this account show the close links that exist between messenger prophecies and certain dream experiences; it also reflects that prophets normally receive their revelations in the temple. When they were not in the temple in person, they visited the temple in their dreams.[41]

The dream report of Malik-Dagan puts into relief yet another aspect of Old Babylonian prophecy. It is clear from the description that Dagan is supposed to speak from within his image. In fact, the author of the letter makes no distinction between the god and his image. It is evident from other texts that the prophet who makes himself the mouthpiece of the god rises and stands before the god, that is, the image of the god, in whose name he delivers an oracle. Note the following description:

---

39 ARM 26 233:9–39.

40 For a likely case of incubation, see ARM 26 232:7–9: "Dagan, your lord, put me to sleep and no one dared to touch me. Dagan spoke to me as follows . . ."; cf. no. 235, possibly a dream received in the temple of Annunitum; and no. 238, a dream by the supervisor of the temple of Itur-mer, presumably received in the temple precinct. ARM 26 236 reports a vision (dream?) received in the temple of Itur-mer.

41 See also ARM 26 227:6–20 (dream about two *muhhû* in the temple of the god Abba); 230 (dialogue between old man and Itur-mer in the stelae-temple of Dagan); 237:8–21 (events in the temple of Belet-ekallim); 240 (temple of Belet-ekallim?).

And the ecstatic (*muhhûm*) rose before (IGI) Dagan and spoke as follows: Shall I never drink clean water? Write to your Lord that he should let me drink clean water![42]

This text renders explicit a procedure that remains implicit in most other texts, in which it is simply said that the prophet "rises" or "stands" in the temple. In all cases, however, the prophet puts himself in front of the god in whose name he speaks and thus makes himself an extension of that god. There is no room for misunderstanding as to who is speaking. That is why we never find, in any of the reports describing a prophecy delivered in the temple, a phrase identifying the divine speaker.[43] The expression *umma* DN-*ma* ("thus god so-and-so") is restricted to letters from gods or their *āpilum.*[44] The only time the prophet finds it necessary to say that god so-and-so has sent him (DN *išpuranni*) is when the prophecy is transmitted to someone outside the sanctuary.[45] The *Botenformel,* then, does not belong to the prophecy properly speaking, but to the introduction to the secondarily transmitted prophecy.

Assyria: Messages from Heaven

When we turn to the Neo-Assyrian prophecies, we enter a different world. The collection tablets contain no indication where the oracles were first delivered. That a number of prophetesses were votaries (*šēlūtu*) need not imply that their oracles were delivered in the temple.[46] In the oracle reports we read of a prophecy given "in the city of Arbela" (SAA 9 6 r. 12) and find one dated prophecy (SAA 9 9 r. 6'–7'). Neo-Assyrian texts containing references to prophetic activities sug-

---

42 ARM 26 215:15–21. See also ARM 26 227:6ff "In my dream Hadnu-El and Iddin-Kubi, the ecstatics, were alive and went before Abba. They spoke as follows . . ." (follows an oracle from the god Abba).

43 Compare the texts mentioned in n. 32. ARM 26 213:7 is no exception, because the phrase *umma Annunītumma* is not a quotation from the prophecy, but an explanation by Queen Šibtu, who sent the letter. The one time one does encouter a self-introduction is A. 1121 + 2731:14–15, 49–50 (= *RA* 78 [1984]: 17–18), but there it serves not to reveal the identity of the divine speaker, but to underline the favors formerly bestowed by the god.

44 See ARM 26 192; 193; 194; and FLP 1674 (= *MARI* 5 [1987]: 235–66, esp. 240).

45 See n. 36.

46 See, e.g., SAA 13 148.

gest that the oracles might occur anywhere, be it inside or—more frequently—outside the temple.[47]

Turning to the oracles themselves, we encounter additional evidence for setting the prophecy outside the temple. The most telling example, in this respect, is an oracle by the woman Bayâ from Arbela, in which the gods Bel, Ištar of Arbela, and Nabû are successively introduced as speakers (SAA 9 1.4). Though Ištar had a famous temple in Arbela, there is not the slightest hint in our records that it contained chapels for the images of Bel and Nabû.[48] We must assume that Bayâ gave her prophecy in one piece in the absence of the images of Bel and Nabû.

There is also internal evidence in the oracle of Bayâ indicating that the audience could not be sure on behalf of which deity she was speaking. Each god had to be identified by a formula of self-introduction. Modern readers would not be aware of the multiplicity of divine voices if it were not for the fact that the gods present themselves with the words "I am Bel" (17'), "I am Ištar of Arbela" (30'), and "I am Nabû, lord of the stylus" (38'). Such formulae of self-introduction are extremely rare in the Old Babylonian prophecies. The only time one does occur, it serves not to identify the god, but to underscore his support of the king in the past.[49] There is reason to believe that the omnipresence of divine self-introduction in the Neo-Assyrian prophecies is not merely a matter of style. The audience needed to hear this, otherwise they would not know which god was speaking. Such ambiguity is not inherent in the situations in which the Old Babylonian prophecies were originally delivered.

---

47 See Nissinen, *References*, passim, but esp. 28 and n. 121; 64–65 (prophets among the military, providing oracles during a royal campaign). See also Simo Parpola, *Letters from Assyrian Scholars to the Kings Esarhaddon and Assurbanipal* (AOAT 5/1; Kevelaer, Germany: Butzon & Bercker; Neukirchen-Vluyn: Neukirchener, 1970), no. 29 r. 7–11. Parpola's no. 317 (= SAA 13 37) shows that Neo-Assyrian prophecies could also be delivered in temples; see Nissinen, *References*, 78–81. Some relevant texts not discussed by Nissinen are now to be found in SAA 13: no. 139 (= Robert Francis Harper, *Assyrian and Babylonian Letters* [London and Chicago: Luzac, 1892–1914], no. 1249); no. 144 (= *CT* 53, no. 969); no. 148 (= *CT* 53, no. 413).

48 See Brigitte Menzel, *Assyrische Tempel: Band 1* (Studia Pohl, Series Maior 10; Rome: Biblical Institute Press, 1981), 6–10.

49 See n. 43. The case of ARM 26 194:3, *umma* ^dUTU-*ma bēl māt*[*im anaku*], is uncertain because of the lacuna in the text and slightly different, as the context is epistolary.

The Neo-Assyrian prophets, then, were apparently not bound to be in the presence of the divine image in order to receive a message from the god. Prophecy occurred regularly outside the sanctuary. The gods resided in heaven, and from there they could reach their human mouthpieces in any number of circumstances.

The Realm of the Divine Actions

A careful reading of the Old Babylonian texts on the one hand, and the Neo-Assyrian texts on the other, reveals a further difference between the two bodies of prophecies. This fourth difference—the last one I discuss in this essay—concerns the way in which the gods come to the aid of the king. Whereas the Old Babylonian gods secure the success of the king by their presence on earth, as auxiliaries of his army, the Neo-Assyrian deities influence the outcome of political and military conflict by an intervention from heaven. In the Old Babylonian prophecies, the battle in which the gods become involved remains within the human horizon; in the Neo-Assyrian texts, however, the battle takes on cosmic dimensions.

Conflicts, often armed, are the traditional area in which the gods are supposed to demonstrate their support of the king. In the Old Babylonian prophecies, the standing expression for the gods' participation in combat is to say that the gods "go" (*alāku*) or "stand" (*izuzzu*) "at the side of" (*ina idi*) the king and his army.[50] They are the "auxiliary troops" (*tillātu*) of the king.[51] The standard formula comes in several variations and elaborations. The gods stand by the king "with [their] strong weapons";[52] they send their "strong weapons" and "nets" to the king, that he may defeat and capture his enemies.[53] The divine intervention leads the king to victory; the gods are with him "in the defeat (of the enemy)" (*ina damdêm*)[54] and "in the triumph (over the enemy)" (*ina lītim*).[55]

Familiar as we are with a tradition in which God is deemed invisible, we tend to assume that the presence of the gods on the battlefield was

---

50 ARM 26 194:27: (Nergal) *ana idika u idi ummânatika izziz*; 207:31–34: (the gods) *ša ina idi bēliya illaku.*

51 ARM 26 207:31.

52 ARM 26 192:17–8: *ina kakkīya dannūtim azazzakkum.*

53 ARM 26 192:6–7; 209:9–10; 233:37ff.

54 ARM 26 194:26.

55 ARM 26 211:15.

an invisible one, perceptible only by its effects. The Old Babylonian reality was probably different, though. Gods accompanied the royal army in the form of images and other visible symbols. Divine images (*iš-ta-ra-tim*) carried by the military are mentioned in a letter by Šamši-Addu.[56] The Mari kings knew the same practice. And when Addu of Aleppo claims that he gave Zimri-Lim "the weapons with which [he] defeated Têmtum" (GIŠ.TUKUL-[MEŠ] *ša itti Têmtim amtahṣu addinakkum*),[57] it must be assumed that the king did in fact receive physical representations of these weapons. We know from other Old Babylonian texts that temples harbored such weapons as objects of veneration.[58] If images of the gods could be paraded in front of the troops, there is no reason why the arms of the gods could not be brought along as well.

The upshot is that the Old Babylonian prophecies picture the intervention of the gods taking place "on the ground," so to speak. Their action does not disrupt the natural framework of the battle.

The interventions of the gods promised in the Neo-Assyrian prophecies are of a different character. Here the gods send their support from heaven, thus disturbing a human conflict with interventions from a different world. A few quotations will suffice to illustrate the point. A fine example is found in an oracle of the god Aššur, recited in an enthronement ritual.

> I heard your cry. I issued forth as a fiery glow from heaven, to hurl down fire and have it devour them. You were standing in their midst, so I removed them from your presence. I drove them up the mountain and rained (hail)stones and fire of heaven upon them. I slaughtered your enemies and filled the river with their blood. Let them see (it) and praise me, for I am Aššur, lord of the gods.[59]

Owing to the intervention of Aššur, the battle acquires a cosmic dimension. The god participates from heaven, and the forces he uses to save the king are from the heavenly realm: lightning and hailstones. The outcome of the battle is determined by transcendent powers.

The Aššur prophecy is not the only one to employ such cosmic imagery. Take the following quotations from an oracle of Ištar of Arbela.

---

56 ARM 1 53 + M. 7340:18; see *MARI* 4 (1985): 316–17, with n. 107.

57 A. 1968 r. 2'–4' (see *MARI* 7 [1993]: 43–45).

58 See, e.g., A. Catagnoti, "Le royaume de Tubâ et ses cultes," in *Florilegium Marianum: Recueil M. Fleury* (Mémoires de *NABU* 1; Paris: SEPOA, 1992), 23–28, esp. 25–26 (offerings for the lance [^{d}*sappum*] of Ištar of Tubâ).

59 SAA 9 3.3 ii 14–25 (trans. Parpola, with one slight change).

> I watch from a golden chamber in the midst of the heavens; I let the lamp of amber shine before Esarhaddon, king of Assyria, and I watch him like the crown of my head. . . . From the great heavens I keep you by your curl. I make smoke rise up on your right side, I kindle fire on your left.[60]

The imagery differs fundamentally from that of the Old Babylonian prophecies. The goddess has her abode in heaven ("a golden chamber in the midst of heaven"), and from there she makes the king stand in the middle of the combat by keeping him by his curl (meaning a lock of hair). Smoke and fire are sent down from heaven to scare his adversaries.

Even the more traditional image of the gods going with the royal troops takes on a different hue in the Neo-Assyrian texts. Ištar of Arbela is said to go "before and behind" the king, which means that her presence surrounds him invisibly.[61] The same message is phrased in other terms when the deity promises that she will "twitter over [the king] and go in circles around [him] like a winged bird ov[er its young]."[62] Such involvement cannot be visualized with the help of images or symbols. The Neo-Assyrian prophets are speaking of a spiritual presence of the gods. They do so, I submit, because their very view of the gods differs from that of their Old Babylonian counterparts. The gods have become transcendent.[63]

Conclusion

The four points of contrast elaborated in this contribution may be summed up, I suggest, in the opposition of immanence versus transcendence. In the Old Babylonian conception, the gods inhabit this world. They speak from their statues, and the support they hold out has an inner-mundane character: they participate in the royal combats on the ground. Their oracles do not transcend the historical situations they address. The prophets that speak on their behalf remain within the socially accepted roles—aside from one or two exceptions.

By Neo-Assyrian times, the gods have their proper habitat in heaven. Temples and temple statues are the symbolic representations

---

60 SAA 9 1.6 iii 23'–29'; iv 26–32.

61 SAA 9 1.1 i 22'–24'.

62 SAA 9 2.3 ii 6'–7'.

63 For other references to divine aid offered to the king, see SAA 9 1.4 ii 20'–26'; 2.2 i 20'–22'; 9:16–17.

of their presence. The gods are free to speak at any place: a prophet need not be in the presence of the divine statue in order to obtain an oracle. Divine involvement in human affairs has likewise a transcendental character. The gods send their help from heaven. Oracles have durative value, transcending the limits of the historical situation in view of which they were originally spoken. The prophets, finally, are members of a cult whose main characteristic is that it transcends the traditional division of roles.

Owing to the distance from which we look at the phenomenon of ancient Near Eastern prophecy, we tend to be especially sensitive to its common characteristics. A closer look reveals important differences between separate bodies of prophetic texts. Such differences should be no cause for wonder, considering the lapse of time between Old Babylonian and Neo-Assyrian prophecy. To the extent this is possible, our view from a distance needs to be counterbalanced by a view from nearby, if we wish to do justice to the historical and local development of the phenomenon of ancient Near Eastern prophecy.

6

The Socioreligious Role of the Neo-Assyrian Prophets

Martti Nissinen

The Neo-Assyrian Evidence for Prophets and Prophecy

The updated list of the ancient Near Eastern documents related to prophecy comprises more than 130 texts, of which about half come from Mari and a little less than half from Assyria.[1] The Neo-Assyrian evidence for prophecy consists of documents of two kinds: the twenty-nine oracles included in the eleven tablets published recently by Simo Parpola,[2] and the haphazard collection of miscellaneous sources consisting of about twenty texts—inscriptions, letters, administrative documents, cultic texts, and a treaty—that allude in one way or another to prophets or their sayings, most of which are included in my recent monograph devoted to these sources.[3] In addition, there are some relevant Neo-Assyrian texts that I failed to analyze in that book: a group of letters, now published by Steven W. Cole and Peter Machinist;[4] a de-

1 For an overview of the sources of the ancient Near Eastern prophecy, see Herbert B. Huffmon, "Ancient Near Eastern Prophecy," *ABD* 5:477–82; Manfred Weippert, "Prophetie im Alten Orient," *NBL* 3:196–200; and compare the list in Martti Nissinen, "Spoken, Written, Quoted, and Invented: Orality and Writtenness in Ancient Near Eastern Prophecy," in *Writings and Speech in Israelite and Ancient Near Eastern Prophecy* (ed. Ehud Ben Zvi and Michael Floyd; SBLSymS; Atlanta: Scholars Press, 1999). The complete collection of these sources will be included in my forthcoming SBLWAW volume, *Prophets and Prophecies from the Ancient Near East.*

2 Simo Parpola, *Assyrian Prophecies* (SAA 9; Helsinki: Helsinki University Press, 1997).

3 Martti Nissinen, *References to Prophecy in Neo-Assyrian Sources* (SAAS 7; Helsinki: Neo-Assyrian Text Corpus Project, 1998), includes analyses of the following texts: Esarhaddon Nin. A i 84–ii 11; Ass. A i 31–ii 26; Assurbanipal A ii 126–iii 26; B v 46–vi 16; T ii 7–24; SAA 2 6 §10; SAA 7 9; SAA 10 109; 111; 284; 294; 352; SAA 13 37 (= *LAS* 317); *ABL* 1217+; *CT* 53 17+; *CT* 53 938.

4 Steven W. Cole and Peter Machinist, *Letters from Priests to the Kings Esarhaddon and Assurbanipal* (SAA 13; Helsinki: Helsinki University Press, 1998), nos. 139; 144;

cree of expenditures in the Aššur Temple from the year 809;[5] as well as a few ritual texts.[6] The prophetic nature of some of these texts is still at issue.

The prominent percentage of Assyrian texts among the sources of prophecy means that no longer can serious study of ancient Near Eastern prophecy be accomplished without taking this material into consideration. Neo-Assyrian documentation of prophecy provides essential insight into the role and image of the prophets as religious specialists and members of the community, and is relevant to our understanding of ancient Near Eastern prophecy as well as of Neo-Assyrian society and religion.

The Assyrian Prophets: *mahhû* and *raggimu*

Basic aspects of the socioreligious role of the Assyrian prophets can be learned from the Neo-Assyrian words for "prophet," *mahhû/mahhūtu* and *raggimu/raggintu.*[7] The word *mahhû/mahhūtu* is equal to *muhhûm/muhhūtum* ([MÍ.]LÚ.GUB.BA), which is one of the most common prophetic designations at Mari[8] and attested elsewhere in various

---

and 148; see the relevant chapter in the introduction to that volume, written by Robert M. Whiting (xvii).

5 Laura Kataja and Robert M. Whiting, *Grants, Decrees, and Gifts of the Neo-Assyrian Period* (SAA 12; Helsinki: Helsinki University Press, 1995), no. 69.

6 I.e., the "Marduk Ordeal" in Alasdair Livingstone, *Court Poetry and Literary Miscellanea* (SAA 3; Helsinki: Helsinki University Press, 1989), no. 34 (duplicate, 35), and the Tammuz and Ištar ritual in Walter Farber, *Beschwörungsrituale an Ištar und Dumuzi: Attī Ištar ša ḫarmaša Dumuzi* (Akademie der Wissenschaften und der Literatur, Veröffentlichungen der orientalischen Kommission 30; Wiesbaden: Franz Steiner, 1977), esp. 140–42 (A IIa:31, 59, *mahhê u mahhūti*). Note also the passage in the Late Babylonian *akītu* ritual reminiscent of prophecy, in F. Thureau-Dangin, *Rituels accadiens* (Paris: Leroux, 1921), 144–45 (lines 434–52), quoted by Karel van der Toorn, "L'Oracle de victoire comme expression prophétique au Proche-Orient ancien," *RB* 94 (1987): 63–97, esp. 93.

7 See Parpola, *Assyrian Prophecies*, xlv–xlvii, with footnotes 212–36 (pp. cii–civ); Beate Pongratz-Leisten, *Herrschaftswissen in Mesopotamien: Formen der Kommunikation zwischen Gott und König im 2. und 1. Jahrtausend v.Chr.* (SAAS 10; Helsinki: Neo-Assyrian Text Corpus Project, 1999), 59–60.

8 The word *muhhûm* is attested in ARM 21 333:34, 43; ARM 22 167:8; ARM 23 446:9, 19; ARM 25 142:13; ARM 26 202:15; 206:5; 215:15; 220:16; 221:19; 221-bis:12, 20, 27; 227:9; 243:7, 13; ARM 27 32:7; A. 1249b+: 2; A. 3165 ii 22; s. ii 3; A. 4676:5; *muhhūtum* in ARM 22 326:9; ARM 26 200:5, 21; 201:9, 15; 237:22; A. 1249b+:6; see Jean-Marie Durand, *Archives Épistolaires de Mari I/1* (ARM 26; Paris: Éditions Recherche sur les Civilisations, 1988), 386–88, 398.

sources, such as omen collections, lexical texts, and administrative documents, from Ur III through the Old Babylonian and Middle Assyrian periods to the Neo-Babylonian.[9] While the use of *mahhû/mahhūtu* in Neo-Assyrian sources is virtually restricted to cultic texts and formal inscriptions,[10] the second designation, *raggimu/raggintu*, appears in administrative texts, personal letters, and colophons of the extant prophecies.[11] This implies that *raggimu/raggintu* was in fact the colloquial equivalent of *mahhû/mahhūtu*, which was probably no longer in use in the seventh century.

Both designations are derived from verbs denoting behavior: *mahhû* from *mahû*, "to become crazy, to go into a frenzy,"[12] and *raggimu* from *ragāmu*, "to cry out, to proclaim." One might ask whether etymologies, notoriously treacherous in defining words, tell anything about the comportment of the prophets. Fortunately, we do not depend on etymology alone when tracing the image of the Mesopotamian prophets with this vocabulary. The verbs in question use their literal meanings when prophetic activities are described.[13] In Mari documents, *mahû*

---

9 *muhhûm*: TCS 1 369:5 (Ur III); MDP 10 7:6, 9; MDP 18 171:14 (Old Babylonian); VS 19 1 i 38 (Middle Assyrian); OECT 1 plate 21:38; YOS 6 18:1, 7, 8, 10; YOS 7 135:6 (Neo-Babylonian); *CT* 38 4:81; Sm 332 r. 5 (Šumma alu); *TDP* 4:30 (Sagig); *DA* 211 r. 12; *MSL* 12 101–2:213; 132:117–18; 158:23; *muhhūtum*: TCL 10 39:11 (Old Babylonian); VS 19 1 i 38 (Middle Assyrian); *CT* 38 4:81 (Šumma alu); *MSL* 12 158:23. See Parpola, *Assyrian Prophecies*, xlv–vi, ciii, nn. 221, 222, 223, 228.

10 Absolute forms are only attested in the ritual texts (SAA 3 34:28; Farber, *Beschwörungsrituale*, 140–42:31, 59), in the Succession Treaty of Esarhaddon (SAA 2 6 §10:117) and in the decree of expenditures from the year 809 (SAA 12 69:29), whereas the royal inscriptions repeatedly use the compound *šipir mahhê*, "prophetic messages" (Esarhaddon Nin A ii 6; Ass A ii 12; Assurbanipal B v 95 [= C vi 127]; T ii 16 [= C i 61]).

11 *raggimu*: SAA 2 6 §10:116; SAA 7 9 r. i 23; SAA 9 3.5 iv 31; [6 r. 11]; SAA 10 109:9; 294 r. 31; *raggintu*: SAA 9 7:1; 10 s. 2; SAA 10 109:9; 352:23, r. 1; SAA 13 37:7.

12 Rather than allophones of a noun of *parrās* pattern (*GAG* §55o, s. 62), *muhhû* and *mahhû* are the Babylonian and Assyrian variants of a D-stem verbal adjective (Parpola, *Assyrian Prophecies*, ciii, n. 219). This makes unnecessary the assumption of a semantic contamination of two different words (Howard Wohl, "The Problem of the *maḫḫû*," *JANESCU* 3 [1970–1971]: 112–18).

13 There are plenty of nonprophetical attestations of both words; cf. 4 R 28:59: *ṣehru imahhi rabû imahhi*, "the small and the great alike go into a frenzy" (cf. Joel 3:1); *BWL* 38:21: *ana ša imhû bēlšu imšû*, "Like one who has gone mad and forgotten his lord"; Esarhaddon Nin A i 41–42: *arkānu ahhēja immahûma mimma ša eli ilāni u amelūti lā ṭāba ēpušūma*, "Afterward my brothers went out of their senses doing everything that is displeasing to the gods and mankind." For a nonprophetical oc-

(N stem) indicates the condition in which the prophets receive and transmit divine words:

ina bīt Annunītim UD.3.KAM *Šēlebum immahhu umma Annunītumma . . .*
In the temple of Annunitum, on the 3rd day, Šelebum went into a frenzy and said: "Thus says Annunitum: (. . .)"[14]

Ahātum amat Dagan-Malik immahhima kīʾam iqbi . . .
Ahatum, a slave girl of Dagan-Malik, went into a frenzy and spoke: (. . .)[15]

[ūmīšum] a Irra-gamil [imma] hêm [umma š] ūma . . .
[On that day] Irra-gamil [went into a fr]enzy. [This is what] he said: (. . .)[16]

Interestingly enough, in a ritual text from Mari, the prophet is said to be deprived of his capacity to prophesy if he maintains an unaltered state of mind:

šumma ina rēš war[him] muhhûm ištaqa[lma] an[a] mahhēʾi[m] ul i[reddû] . . .
If by the end of the mo[nth] the *muhhûm* maintains his equili[brium] and is not a[ble] t[o] prophes[y] (. . .)[17]

In Neo-Assyrian sources, again, the verb *ragāmu* is regularly used of prophetic performance:

Tašmētu-ērēš [raggimu annītu ina lib]bi Arbail irt[ugum]
Tašmetu-ereš, the [prophet], prop[hesied this i]n Arbela.[18]

[a] sseme mā pānāt nēpēšē annūti ragginti tartugūmu
ana Damqî mār šatammi taqṭi[bi m] ā . . .
[I] have heard that, before these rituals, a prophetess had prophesied, saying to Damqî, the son of the chief administrator: "(. . .)"[19]

---

currence of *ragāmu*, see SAA 13 157:24: *mā Nabû-abu-daʾʾin nuhatimmu irtugum,* "Then Nabû-abu-daʾʾin, the cook, cried out."

14 ARM 26 213:5–7.

15 ARM 26 214:6–7.

16 ARM 26 222:12–14.

17 A. 3165 ii 21–23 (Ritual of Ištar, text 2); for the restoration and translation, see Durand, *Archives,* 386–87; Jean-Marie Durand and Michaël Guichard, "Les rituels de Mari," in *Florilegium marianum III: Recueil d'études à la mémoire de Marie-Thérèse Barrelet* (ed. Dominique Charpin and Jean-Marie Durand; Mémoires de *NABU* 4; Paris: SEPOA, 1997), 19–78, esp. 54, 58.

18 SAA 9 6 r. 11–12. The title of Tašmetu-ereš follows the professional determinative LÚ, which is partially broken but clearly visible (see the photograph in Parpola, *Assyrian Prophecies,* plate viii); however, the title itself is totally broken away.

19 SAA 10 352:22–25.

Mullissu-abu-uṣri raggintu ša kuzippī ša šarri ana māt Akkadî tūbilūni [ina] bēt ili tartug[u]m . . .

Mullissu-abu-uṣri, the prophetess who conveyed the king's clothes to the land of Akkad, prophesied [in] the temple: (. . .)[20]

As demonstrated by the above examples, both *mahû* and *ragāmu* tend to introduce direct divine speech, which indicates that, semantically, they encompass both aspects of the oral performance of the prophet, that is, the distinct behavior and the act of speech. In the Hebrew Bible, prophetic performance is expressed with derivatives of the root *nbʾ*, which means proclamation of divine words, often implying an appearance in an altered state of mind and, hence, providing a semantic equivalent of *mahû* and *ragāmu.*[21]

In addition to the prophetic designations, the behavior and social location of the Assyrian prophets can be contextualized by comparison with related groups of people and their behaviors. It is revealing that in lexical lists as well as cultic and administrative texts, *raggimu* and *mahhû* are consistently associated with people like *zabbu* 'frenzied one', *kalû* 'chanter', *munambû* 'lamentation singer', *lallaru* 'wailer', *assinnu* and *kurgarrû* 'man-woman'—all devotees of Ištar with appearance and conduct different from the average citizen. For example:

la-bar	=	*kalû*	"chanter"
gala.mah	=	*kalamāhu* (ŠU-*hu*)	"chief chanter"
i-lu-di	=	*munambû*	"lamentation singer"
i-lu-a-li	=	*lallaru*	"wailer"
lú.gub-ba	=	*mahhû*	"prophet"
lú.ní-zu-ub	=	*zabbu*	"frenzied one"
kur-gar-ra	=	*kurgarrû* (ŠU-*u*)	"man-woman"
ur-sal	=	*assinnu*	"man-woman"
lú.giš.bala-šu-du$_7$	=	*nāš pilaqqi*	"carrier of spindel"[22]

[20] SAA 13 37:7–10.

[21] E.g., Num 11:24–30; 1 Sam 10:10–13; 19:20; 1 Kgs 18:29; 22:10; Joel 3:1. In the semantics of Biblical Hebrew, however, use of the word family *nbʾ* is restricted to prophetic activities.

[22] *MSL* 12 102–3:209–17 (M. Civil et al., *The Series lú = ša and Related Texts* [MSL 12; Rome: Pontificium Institutum Biblicum, 1969], 102–3); the designation *nāš pilaqqi* is equal to *assinnu* and *kurgarrû*. Cf. the decree of expenditures from Mari (ARM 21 333:42–44 = ARM 23 446:18–20): 1 *ṣubātum išārum Jadīda lillatum* 1 *ṣubātum išārum Ēa-maṣi muhhû Itūr-Mēr* 1 *ṣubātum išārum Šarrum-dāri nārum,* "one ordinary garment for Yadida 'the crazy woman,' one ordinary garment for Ea-maṣi, prophet of Itur-Mer, one ordinary garment for Šarrum-dari, the chanter." Note

aštakkan kurummāti ana zabbī zabbāti mahhê u mahhūti

I have placed breads for the frenzied men and women, for prophets and prophetesses.[23]

10 *emār* 4 *sât* 5 *qa Aššūr-apla-iddina ina* UD.2.KÁM *ana kurummat mahhuʾē mahhuʾāte u* LÚ.SAL.MEŠ *ša bēt Iltār*

10 homers 4 seah 5 liters (of barley)[24] for Aššūr-apla-iddina on the 2nd day, for the food rations of the prophets, prophetesses, and the *assinnu*'s (?) of the Ištar temple (of Kar-Tukulti-Ninurta).[25]

The uncertain gender of some Assyrian prophets—especially Bayâ, whose gender even the scribe of the tablet SAA 9 1 could not decide[26]—creates a link to the *assinnu* and the *kurgarrû,* whose gender role the goddess had changed permanently;[27] this is not surprising given that two of the Mari prophets, Šelebum and Ili-haznaya, are explicitly designated as *assinnu.*[28] On the other hand, an established connection exists between prophets and the seers and visionaries called *šabrû* and *šāʾilu,* whose expertise is closely related to that of the prophets. The only Neo-Assyrian occurrence[29] of *šāʾilu* (*amat ili*) occurs in the Succession Treaty of Esarhaddon, where it is listed together with *raggimu* and *mahhû* and may, rather than designating a specific

---

that the prophet is mentioned in association with a woman, whose title *lillatum* probably designates ecstatic behavior, and with a chanter comparable to *kalû.*

23 Farber, *Beschwörungsrituale,* 142:59; cf. 140:31.

24 On the basis of the preceding paragraphs (lines i 17, 21, 23, 31, 33), which regularly give *šeʾu* (ŠE) as the product delivered.

25 VS 19 1 i 37–39 (Helmut Freydank, "Zwei Verpflegungstexte aus Kār-Tukultī-Ninurta," *AoF* 1 [1974]: 55–89, esp. 60). The reading *assinnu* is based on Freydank's copy, which shows clear traces of the sign SAL (= MÍ) between the signs LÚ and MEŠ (Helmut Freydank, *Mittelassyrische Rechtsurkunden und Verwaltungstexte* [Vorderasiatische Schriftdenkmäler 19; Berlin: Akademie-Verlag, 1976], plate 1).

26 SAA 9 1.4 ii 40 gives the name incongruously as MÍ.*ba-ia-a* DUMU URU.*arba-ìl,* "the woman Bayâ, son of Arbela." The name has both male and female occurrences in Neo-Assyrian sources (see M. Nissinen and M.-C. Perroudon, "Bāia," *PNA* 1/II:253). In the case of Ištar-la-tašiyaṭ, the masculine and divine determinatives [md] are written over the originally written MÍ (SAA 9 1.1 i 28); it is not clear whether this is an error of the scribe or indicates uncertainty about the gender of the prophet.

27 For *assinnu* and *kurgarrû,* see, e.g., Gwendolyn Leick, *Sex and Eroticism in Mesopotamian Literature* (London and New York: Routledge, 1994), 157–69; Martti Nissinen, *Homoeroticism in the Biblical World* (Minneapolis: Fortress Press, 1998), 28–36.

28 ARM 26 197:4; 198:3; 213:6; M. 11299:8 (Šelebum); 212:5; M. 11299:13 (Ili-haznaya). See Durand, *Archives,* 399.

29 I.e., besides the entry in the lexical list in *MSL* 12 233:33, where [LÚ.*ša-i*]-*lu* appears as a category of its own.

role or profession, be a general appellation for practitioners of different kinds of noninductive divination.[30] The *šabrû*, equated with *raggimu* in a lexical list[31] and appearing in close connection with both *maḫḫû* and *zabbu* in other texts,[32] is a visionary whose realm apparently consists of dreams and their interpretation.[33] A dream of a *šabrû* with many affinities with prophecy is reported in Assurbanipal's Prism B, following the quotation of an oracle that is best explained as prophetic.[34]

The outcome of the etymological and lexical examination is that the Assyrian prophets were proclaimers of divine words who formed part of the community of devotees of Ištar. They found their nearest colleagues among practitioners of noninductive divination and among people whose more or less frenzied behavior, eventually perceived as odd by the majority of the population, corresponded to their role in the worship of the goddess.

The Prophets and the Goddess

The determinative factor in the socioreligious role of the Assyrian prophets is without doubt their affiliation with the goddess Ištar and worship of her.[35] Prophets act as mouthpieces of that goddess in her various manifestations; in Neo-Assyrian texts, Mullissu cannot be separated from Ištar as a divine being.[36] The prophets also live under the

---

30 SAA 2 6 §10:117; cf. Nissinen, *References*, 160–61.

31 *MSL* 12 226:134: lú.šabra (PA.AL) = ŠU-*u* = *rag-gi-*[*mu*].

32 *CT* 38 4 81–82: *šumma ina* URU LÚ.GUB.BA.MEŠ MIN (= *ma-ʾ-du*) [. . .] *šumma ina* URU MÍ.GUB.BA.MEŠ MIN [. . .], "If there are many prophets in the city, [. . .]; if there are many prophetesses in the city, [. . .]; 87–88: *šumma ina* URU *šab-ru*.MEŠ MIN [. . .] *šumma ina* URU *šab-ra-tu*$_4$ MIN [. . .], "If there are many frenzied men in the city, [. . .], if there are many frenzied women in the city, [. . .]"; *LKA* 29d ii 2: *zabbu liqbâkkima šabrû lišannakki*, "Let the *zabbu* tell you, the *šabrû* repeat it to you."

33 For *šabrû*, see *CAD* Š/1 15; Huffmon, "Ancient Near Eastern Prophecy," 5:480; Parpola, *Assyrian Prophecies*, xlvi–xlvii; Nissinen, *References*, 56.

34 Assurbanipal B v 49–76; see Manfred Weippert, "Assyrische Prophetien der Zeit Asarhaddons und Assurbanipals," in *Assyrian Royal Inscriptions: New Horizons in Literary, Ideological, and Historical Analysis* (ed. F. M. Fales; OAC 17; Rome: Istituto per l'Oriente, 1981), 71–115, esp. 97–98; Nissinen, *References*, 53–54; Pongratz-Leisten, *Herrschaftswissen*, 120–22.

35 As to the following, see the detailed documentation of Parpola, *Assyrian Prophecies*, xlvii–xlviii, with footnotes on pp. civ–cvi.

36 See Brigitte Menzel, *Assyrische Tempel: Untersuchungen zu Kult, Administration und Personal* (Studia Pohl, Series Major 10/I; Rome: Biblical Institute Press, 1981),

aegis of the goddess. Their association with other devotees of Ištar in the above-mentioned lexical lists and cultic texts, as well as their mention as recipients of food rations in the Ištar temple of the Middle Assyrian period, shows this fact conclusively. The prophets' permanent attachment to the temples is further documented by one oracle of the corpus, spoken by a votaress (*šēlūtu*) donated to the goddess by the king.[37] Many prophets have names related to the ideology of Ištar worship. These probably are not birth names but given when the prophetic role was assumed.[38]

As proclaimers of the word of Ištar, the prophets acted *as* Ištar. The primary role of the prophets as intermediaries between the divine and the human spheres reflects the role of Ištar/Mullissu as the mediator between the gods and the king, as demonstrated by a prophetic oracle and a letter containing a report of a prophetic utterance:

ina puhur ilāni kalāmi aqṭibi balāṭaka
dannā rittāja lā urammâka ina pān ilāni
naggalapāja harruddā ittanaššāka ana kāša
ina š[*apt*]*ēja ētanarriš balāṭaka* [. . .]

In the assembly of all the gods I have spoken for your life.
My arms are strong and will not cast you off before the gods.
My shoulders are always ready to carry you, you in particular.
I keep desiring your life with my l[ip]s [. . .][39]

64–65, 116; Manfred Weippert, "Die Bildsprache der neuassyrischen Prophetie," in Helga Weippert, Klaus Seybold, and Manfred Weippert, *Beiträge zur prophetischen Bildsprache in Israel und Assyrien* (OBO 64; Freiburg, Switzerland: Universitätsverlag; Göttingen: Vandenhoeck & Ruprecht, 1985), 55–93, esp. 64; cf. SAA 3 7:11–12; SAA 9 2.4 ii 30; SAA 9 7 r. 6; and especially SAA 9 9, in which Mullissu and Lady (Ištar) of Arbela speak in the first-person singular as one divine being. Mullissu also appears as the one speaking in SAA 9 1.5 iii 4; SAA 9 5:3; and SAA 9 7:2, 12.

37 SAA 9 1.7. Moreover, it is possible that the fragment SAA 13 148 is a remainder of another votaress's prophecy report: [. . .]-*ia* [. . .] *šēlūtu* [*ša*] *Issār* [*ša*] *Arbail ši*[*pirt*]*i* [*ann*]*ītu ana š*[*arri bēl īja* . . .] *Issār* [. . .], "[. . .-]ya, votaress [of] Ištar [of] Arbela [reported] [th]is mes[sag]e for the ki[ng, my lord]: '[. . .] Ištar [. . .]'" It is not clear, however, whether this votaress had actually uttered the divine word in question, or just reports it to the king; cf. Parpola, *Assyrian Prophecies*, lxxvii; Whiting, introduction to Cole and Machinist, *Letters*, xvii.

38 E.g., *Ilūssa-āmur,* "I have seen her divinity"; *Issār-bēlī-da''ini,* "Ištar, strengthen my lord!"; *Issār-lā-tašīyat,* "Do not neglect Ištar!"; *Sinqīša-āmur,* "I have seen her distress"; see Parpola, *Assyrian Prophecies,* il–lii.

39 SAA 9 9:16–20; cf. the similar language used in SAA 3 13.

[anāku] Bēl ētarba issi Mu[ll]issu asillim
Aššūr-bāni-apli šar māt Aššūr ša turabbīni [l] ā tapallah
[anā] ku Bēl artēanki Aššūr-bāni-apli ina māti ša kēnu šû adi mātišu artēanki

[I] am Bel, I have entered and reconciled with Mullissu.
Assurbanipal, king of Assyria whom she raised: Fear not!
I am Bel, I have had mercy on you (f.). Assurbanipal is in a country which remains loyal. I have had mercy on you, together with his country.[40]

While the first quotation presents the goddess(es)[41] as intercessor(s) before the divine council, the second is the word of Bel, who declares his reconciliation with Assurbanipal upon the intercession of Mullissu who, for her part, stands on behalf of the king. Hence, the prophetic message appears as the earthly representation and counterpart of the divine intermediation of the goddess in the heavenly council. The prophet, impersonating the goddess, is the channel through which the benefit of her intercession, the divine reconciliation, is bestowed upon the king.

The closest textual parallels with Neo-Assyrian prophecies are found among poetry, hymns, and mystical works pertaining to the cult of different deities, but especially to that of Ištar. These show the prophets' familiarity with this literature and the associated cultic performances. In addition to the mythological compositions like Adapa and Gilgameš,[42] the royal and cultic poetry collected in SAA 3 provides an abundance of affinities with prophecy, especially

1. in hymns and prayers of Assurbanipal,[43] especially in the Dialogue between Assurbanipal and Nabû (SAA 3 13), which is both substantially and historically closely related to SAA 9 9 and was probably written by the same hand;[44]

---

40 SAA 13 139:1–9. The source in question is the letter of Aššur-hamatu'a, who begins with the word of Bel and attaches additional information. Hence, the letter gives an account of a prophetic appearance without being a report of prophecy in the strict sense.

41 The divine "I" in this oracle is spoken by Ištar and Mullissu as one divine being; cf. above, n. 36.

42 See Parpola, *Assyrian Prophecies*, cv, n. 246.

43 SAA 3 1; 2; 3; 7; 12; 13.

44 See Parpola, *Assyrian Prophecies*, lxxi. This text is often discussed together with the prophecies; cf. Meindert Dijkstra, *Gods voorstelling: Predikatieve expressie van zelfopenbaring in oudoosterse teksten en Deutero-Jesaja* (Dissertationes Neerlandicae, Series Theologica 2; Kampen: Kok, 1980), 147–48; Weippert, "Assyrische Prophetien"; idem, "Bildsprache"; Martti Nissinen, "Die Relevanz der neuassyrischen Prophetie für die alttestamentliche Forschung," in *Mesopotamica—Ugaritica—Biblica: Festschrift für Kurt Bergerhof* (ed. Manfried Dietrich and Oswald Loretz; AOAT 232, Kevelaer, Germany: Butzon & Bercker; Neukirchen-Vluyn: Neukirchener,

2. in the letters from gods (or responses to *Gottesbriefe*), which are not prophecy as such, but employ confusingly similar language;[45]
3. in mystical works like SAA 3 37 and 39;[46] and
4. in the love lyrics of Nabû and Tašmetu (SAA 3 14).[47]

An open question is to what extent the literary parallels between prophecies and cultic literature go back to the scribes by whom the prophecy reports were formulated; in any case, similar use of language in both types of sources is not just a stylistic matter but the vehicle for expression of an essentially similar ideology.

Among the cult centers of Ištar, Arbela is by far the most important source of prophecy. If the letter of the temple official Nabû-reši-išši reporting an appearance of a prophetess was sent from Arbela, as suggested by the letter's greeting formula,[48] it only proves the assumption, probable anyway, that prophecies were uttered in the temple of Ištar of Arbela. Seven out of fifteen prophets known by personal names are Arbela-based: Ahat-abiša (SAA 9 1.8), Bayâ (SAA 9 1.4; [2.2]), Dunnaša-amur (SAA 9 9 and 10), Issar-la-tašiyaṭ (SAA 9 1.1), La-dagil-ili (SAA 9 1.10; 2.3 and 3), Sinqiša-amur (SAA 9 1.2; [2.5]), and Tašmetu-ereš (SAA 9 6). The words of Ištar of Arbela were proclaimed even by prophets elsewhere;[49] a special devotion to that city is expressed by the prophetess Remutti-Allati, who comes from Dara-ahuya, an unidentifiable locality "in the mountains" (*birti šaddâni*), proclaiming the words "Arbela rejoices!"[50]

The dominance of Ištar of Arbela does not, however, prevent the

---

1993), 217–58. Pongratz-Leisten (*Herrschaftswissen*, 75) puts forward the idea that SAA 3 13 is a literary creation inspired by the prophecies ("eine literarische Kreation in Anlehnung an die Gattung der Prophetensprüche").

45 SAA 3 44–47; cf. Dijkstra, *Gods voorstelling*, 145–69; Weippert, "Assyrische Prophetien," 72, 112; Livingstone, *Court Poetry*, xxx. For the "correspondence" of Assurbanipal with Aššur, see the comprehensive analysis in Pongratz-Leisten, *Herrschaftswissen*, 240–65.

46 Cf. Parpola, *Assyrian Prophecies*, c, n. 175; cv, n. 248.

47 See Martti Nissinen, "Love Lyrics of Nabû and Tašmetu: An Assyrian Song of Songs?" in *"Und Mose schrieb dieses Lied auf": Studien zum Alten Testament und zum Alten Orient, Festschrift für Oswald Loretz* (ed. Manfried Dietrich and Ingo Kottsieper; AOAT 250, Münster: Ugarit-Verlag, 1998), 585–634, esp. 602, n. 75; 608, n. 103; 613, n. 131; 614, n. 138.

48 SAA 13 144:1–9; cf. the note of Karen Radner in Cole and Machinist, *Letters*, 116.

49 SAA 9 2.4: Urkittu-šarrat from Calah.

50 SAA 9 1.3 ii 12.

prophets from proclaiming the words of other deities. To all appearances, the prophet La-dagil-ili speaks on behalf of both Aššur and Ištar in the collection SAA 9 3,[51] and a short oracle of the prophet(ess) Bayâ (SAA 9 1.4) includes self-predications of three deities, Bel, Ištar, and Nabû. While most of the prophets, as devotees of Ištar, represent the motherly aspect of the divine, manifested as nursing the king and as fighting for him,[52] it is convenient for a prophet to act as the mouthpiece of Aššur when it comes to the covenant between the king and the main god of Assyria.[53] Furthermore, when a Babylonian scholar quotes prophecy, he presents it as the words of Bel, that is, Marduk of Babylon,[54] and when affairs of the city of Harran are concerned, the Harranean deities Nikkal and Nusku speak.[55] All this implies a functional or aspectual, rather than "polytheistic," concept of God, which enabled the prophets to speak the words of the appropriate manifestation of the divine in a given situation. Accordingly, the Assyrian prophets were not divided into competing groups advocating specific deities, and their basic role as devotees of Ištar by no means prevented them from acting in temples of other gods.

As a matter of fact, the presence of prophets in temples other than those of Ištar is well documented. Adad-ahu-iddina writes the king about an appearance of the prophetess Mullissu-abu-uṣri in the temple in which he is employed—most probably Ešarra, the Aššur temple in Assur[56]—and in a decree for the maintenance of the same temple from the year 809, prophetesses (*mahhâtu*) are mentioned in a para-

---

51 See Nissinen, "Spoken, Written, Quoted, and Invented."

52 E.g., SAA 9 1.6 iii 15–22, iv 5–10; SAA 9 2.5 iii 29–34; SAA 9 7:14–r. 11; cf. SAA 3 13 r. 6–10. See Weippert, "Bildsprache," 62–64; Nissinen, "Relevanz," 242–47.

53 The oracle in SAA 9 3.3 ii 10–25 is followed by a double ritual instruction (lines 26–32). It is not compulsory to interpret the oracle as *the* document of the covenant, as I and many others have done (Nissinen, *References*, 28). It is clear that *annû šulmu ša ina pān ṣalme*, "This is the oracle of peace (placed) before the statue" (line 26), refers to the tablet on which the prophecy is written. However, the continuation *ṭuppi adê anniu ša Aššūr . . . ina pān šarri errab*, "This covenant tablet of Aššur enters the king's presence" (lines 27–28), does not necessarily refer to the same tablet; see Pongratz-Leisten, *Herrschaftswissen*, 77–80.

54 SAA 10 111; see Nissinen, *References*, 96–101.

55 *ABL* 1217; *CT* 53 17; see Nissinen, *References*, 122.

56 SAA 13 37 (= *LAS* 317); see Simo Parpola, *Letters from Assyrian Scholars to the Kings Esarhaddon and Assurbanipal*, pt. 2: *Commentary and Appendices* (AOAT 5/2; Kevelaer, Germany: Butzon & Bercker; Neukirchen-Vluyn: Neukirchener, 1983), 329; Nissinen, *References*, 78–81; Pongratz-Leisten, *Herrschaftswissen*, 83–84.

graph concerning the "divine council" (*puhur ilāni*).[57] When it comes to the Babylonian *akītu*-ritual, a prophet (*mahhû*) appears in a genuinely prophetic function as a "bringer of news" (*mupassiru*) to Zarpanitu, the spouse of Marduk, in the so-called Marduk Ordeal text.[58] Everything points to the conclusion that while the Ištar worship in Arbela was undoubtedly the nerve center of prophecy, the network of prophets extended to other cities, where they represented their patroness even in temples of other deities.

The special devotion of Assyrian prophets to Ištar is compatible with the significance of the goddesses, often manifestations of Ištar, in the prophetic documents from Ešnunna (Kititum)[59] and Mari (Annunitum, Ištar of Bišra, Diritum, Belet-ekallim, Belet-biri, Hišamitum, Ninhursag).[60] There is, however, no overall dedication of the prophets to the goddess in Mari documents, in which the role of male deities (Dagan, Šamaš, Adad, Itur-Mer, Nergal, Ea, Abba)[61] in prophecies is clearly more manifest than in Assyria. Moreover, while the prophets in the Neo-Assyrian sources are never called "*raggintu* of Ištar" or the like, the Mari prophets tend to be associated with a specific deity, for example, Lupahum, *āpilum* of Dagan.[62] This probably demonstrates the

57 SAA 12 69:27–31; cf. Kataja and Whiting, *Grants*, xxxii. The divine council plays an important role in SAA 9 9:16: *ina puhur ilāni kalāmi aqṭibi balāṭaka*, "In the assembly of all the gods I have spoken for your life"; cf. SAA 3 13:26: *pîja ammiu ša ṭābu iktanarrabka ina puhur ilāni rabûti*, "My pleasant mouth shall ever bless you in the assembly of the great gods." The letter of Aššur-hamatuʾa (SAA 13 139) contains an oracle in which Bel reconciles with Mullissu, who has interceded on behalf of Assurbanipal, presumably before the divine council; see above.

58 SAA 3 34:28 (= SAA 3 35:31): *mahhû ša ina pān Bēlet-Bābili illakūni mupassiru šû ana irtīša ibakki illak*, "The prophet who goes before the Lady of Babylon is a bringer of news; weeping he goes toward her." For this text (and for reservations about calling it the "Marduk Ordeal"), see Tikva Frymer-Kensky, "The Tribulations of Marduk: The So-Called 'Marduk Ordeal Text,'" *JAOS* 103 (1983): 131–41.

59 FLP 1674 and 2064; see Maria deJong Ellis, "The Goddess Kititum Speaks to King Ibalpiel: Oracle Texts from Ishchali," *MARI* 5 (1987): 235–66.

60 Annunitum: ARM 22 326; 26 198; 212; 213; 214; 237; Ištar of Bišra: ARM 26 237; Diritum: ARM 26 199; 208; Belet-ekallim: ARM 26 209; 211 (?); 237; 240; Belet-biri: ARM 26 238; Hišamitum: ARM 26 195; Ninhursag: ARM 22 167 (cf. A. 4676); 26 219. Note especially the role of the prophets in the rituals of Ištar (A. 3165; A. 1249b+); cf. Durand and Guichard, "Rituels de Mari."

61 Dagan: ARM 25 15; 26 196; 197; 199; 202; 205; 209; 210; 215; 220; 221; 223; 232; 233; A. 3796; M. 11436; T. 82; Šamaš: ARM 26 194; 414; Adad: ARM 25 142; A. 1121+; 1968; Itur-Mer: ARM 21 333; 23 446; 26 236; Nergal: ARM 21 333; 23 446 (26 222?); Ea: ARM 26 208; Abba: ARM 26 227.

62 ARM 26 199:5; A. 3796:4–5; M. 11436:4. There are plenty of similar cases:

prophet's attachment to the temple of a particular god, which as such does not exclude proclaiming the words of other deities, even though this appears to be exceptional at Mari.[63]

The reason for the different significance of the goddess in these two corpora may be sought primarily in the special role of Ištar in the amalgamation of Assyrian imperial ideology with Assyrian religion, which reached a climax in the Sargonid era.[64] However, the sparse documentation shows the elementary connection of prophecy and the cult of Ištar in her various manifestations in different parts of Mesopotamia throughout the ages, which speaks against the much-debated theory of Mesopotamian prophecy as a product of Western influence.[65] Without speculating on the "origin" of prophecy in cultural and geographic terms, if there is an origin, one might note the prominent role of male deities in the few West Semitic documents of prophecy and other oracular activity,[66] and ask whether the relatively

---

Qišatum, *āpilum* of Dagan (ARM 25 15:9); Išhi-Dagan, *āpilum* of Dagan of Ṣubatum (T. 82:3–4); *āpilum* of Dagan of Tuttul (ARM 26 209:6); *āpilum* of Belet-ekallim (ARM 26 209:15); Qišti-Diritim, *āpilum* of Diritum (ARM 26 208:5–6); *āpilum* of Šamaš (ARM 26 194:2); Atamrum, *āpilum* of Šamaš (ARM 26 414:29–30); *āpilum* of Ninhursag (ARM 26 219:5); *āpilum* of Marduk (ARM 26 371:9); Abiya, *āpilum* of Adad (A. 1968:3); Annu-tabni, *muhhūtum* of Annunitum (ARM 22 326:9–10); *muhhûm* of Dagan (ARM 26 220:16–17; 221:9; 243:13 [pl.]); Irra-gamil, *muhhûm* of Nergal (ARM 21 333:34 = ARM 23 446:9); Ea-maṣi, *muhhûm* of Itur-Mer (ARM 21 333:43 = ARM 23 446:19); Ea-mudammiq, *muhhûm* of Ninhursag (ARM 22 167:8; A. 4676:5–6); *muhhûm* of Adad (ARM 25 142:13); *muhhû* of Ami of Hubšalum (ARM 27 32:7); Ili-haznaja, *assinnu* of Annunitum (ARM 26 212:5–6).

63 In addition to the word of his patron god Dagan, Lupahum seems to deliver an oracle of the goddess Diritum in ARM 26 199:29–40. Moreover, Iddin-ili, the priest (*šangûm*) of Itur-Mer, reports a dream of his in which he receives a word of Belet-biri (ARM 26 238).

64 See Parpola, *Assyrian Prophecies*, xxxvi–xliv.

65 This theory, put forward by Hayim Tadmor, "The Aramaization of Assyria: Aspects of Western Impact," in *Mesopotamien und seine Nachbarn: Politische und kulturelle Wechselbeziehungen im Alten Vorderasien vom 4. bis 1. Jahrtausend v. Chr.* (ed. Hans-Jörg Nissen and Johannes Renger; Berliner Beiträge zum Vorderen Orient 1; Berlin: Dietrich Reimer, 1982), 449–70, esp. 458, and supported by, e.g., Manfred Hutter, *Religionen in der Umwelt des Alten Testaments I: Babylonier, Syrer, Perser* (Studienbücher Theologie 4/1; Stuttgart: Kohlhammer, 1996), 107, and Abraham Malamat, "The Cultural Impact of the West (Syria-Palestine) on Mesopotamia in the Old Babylonian Period," *AoF* 24 (1997): 310–19, esp. 315–17, has been objected to by, e.g., Alan Millard, "La prophétie et l'écriture—Israël, Aram, Assyrie," *RHR* 202 (1985): 125–44, esp. 133–34, and most emphatically and conclusively by Parpola, *Assyrian Prophecies*, xiv. Cf. also Pongratz-Leisten, *Herrschaftswissen*, 49–51.

66 E.g., the Zakkur Inscription, the Deir ʿAlla Inscription, the Ammonite Cita-

lesser prominence of the goddess in the prophetic documents of Mari is due to socioreligious circumstances and traditions different from those of imperial Assyria.

The Prophets and the King

Apart from the biblical narratives about prophets having an immediate communication with the kings of Israel or Judah—which may have happened less often than one would have expected[67]—at least one ancient Near Eastern source hints at such encounters, namely the letter of the well-known Babylonian astrologer Bel-ušezib to the king Esarhaddon. Bel-ušezib wonders why Esarhaddon, following his coronation, has summoned "prophets and prophetesses" (*raggimānu raggimātu*) instead of him and in spite of the services he has provided for Esarhaddon during the civil war preceding his rise to power.[68]

This reference is unique in ancient Near Eastern sources, and Bel-ušezib's tone expresses his astonishment and jealousy, as if it were exceptional for prophets to be honored by the king's summons. It is not certain that this reference indicates a face-to-face rendezvous between the prophets and the king. The "summoning" (*rēšu našû*) primarily means employing: the life of a scholar depended on the king's use of his services, and Bel-ušezib is furious because Esarhaddon, at the beginning of his rule, has made use of the prophets' services before consulting the skilled and loyal Babylonian astrologer.

The Mari archives provide, to the best of my knowledge, no record

---

del Inscription, etc.; cf. André Lemaire, "Oracles, propagande et littérature dans les royaumes araméens et transjordaniens (IXe–VIIIe s. av. n.è.)," in *Oracles et prophéties dans l'antiquité: Actes du Colloque de Strasbourg, 15–17 Juin 1995* (ed. Jean-Georges Heintz; Université des sciences humaines de Strasbourg, Travaux du Centre de recherche sur le Proche-Orient et la Grèce antiques 15; Paris: De Boccard, 1997), 171–93.

67 These encounters happen between the anonymous prophet and Jeroboam (1 Kgs 13:1–10); Elijah and Ahab (1 Kgs 18:16–20, 41); Micaiah and Ahab/Jehoshaphat (1 Kgs 22:1–28); Elijah and Ahaziah (2 Kgs 1); Elisha and Ben-Hadad, king of Damascus (2 Kgs 8:7–15); Isaiah and Ahaz (Isa 7); Isaiah and Hezekiah (Isa 37–39 = 2 Kgs 19–20) and Jeremiah and Zedekiah (Jer 34:1–7; 37:17–21; 38:14–28). Jeremiah 21; 36; 37:1–10 are not direct encounters, and, in Jer 22, the prophet is ordered by God to go to the king, but the encounter never takes place.

68 SAA 10 109:8–16; cf. Nissinen, *References*, 89–95. For Bel-ušezib and his correspondence, see Manfried Dietrich, *Die Aramäer Südbabyloniens in der Sargonidenzeit (700–648)* (AOAT 7; Kevelaer, Germany: Butzon & Bercker; Neukirchen-Vluyn: Neukirchener, 1970), 62–68.

of a situation in which a prophet met the king in person; at best, the prophet proclaimed at the gate of the palace, as the anonymous prophet of Marduk in Babylon, delivering a message to the Assyrian king Išme-Dagan, who had received asylum from Hammurapi, king of Babylon.[69] The meager evidence does not allow conclusions about whether direct encounters between the prophets and the king really took place at Mari, and if so, how often, but the existing sources give the impression that while King Zimri-Lim maintained close contact with practitioners of extispicy,[70] he was not active in consulting prophets. Even dreamers and visionaries seem to have communicated their messages more directly to the king than the prophets, whose words were usually conveyed to him by officials from different parts of the kingdom or by women of the court, especially by Queen Šibtu and other royal women (Addu-duri, Inib-šina).[71] Even in Assyria, the kings did not carry on a correspondence with the prophets; however, the transmission of prophetic messages differed from that in Mari. In Assyria, prophecies apparently were seldom reported in letters of court officials, but they were transmitted to the king in reports, the contents of which were limited to the oracle proper. In some cases, these reports were deposited in the royal archives.[72] This implies a higher esteem for prophecies, which, in this procedure, were considered on a par with astrological and extispicy reports.

Both the oracles proper and the references to them in the royal inscriptions make it plain that the Assyrian kings, at least Esarhaddon and Assurbanipal, like Zimri-Lim, received prophecies during their military campaigns. There may even have been prophets at the front,[73] but prophecies uttered elsewhere and transmitted to the king by a

---

69 ARM 26 371; see Dominique Charpin, "Le contexte historique et géographique des prophéties dans les textes retrouvés à Mari," *BCSMS* 23 (1992): 21–31, esp. p. 28–29.

70 See Pongratz-Leisten, *Herrschaftswissen*, 137–54.

71 For the transmission of prophecies at Mari, see Jack M. Sasson, "The Posting of Letters with Divine Messages," in *Florilegium Marianum II, Mémorial M. Birot* (Mémoires de *NABU* 3; Paris: SEPOA, 1994), 299–316; Karel van der Toorn, "Old Babylonian Prophecy between the Oral and the Written," *JNSL* 24 (1998): 55–70.

72 For this procedure, see Nissinen, "Spoken, Written, Quoted, and Invented."

73 This is suggested by accounts of kings in the royal inscriptions having received prophecies during battles, as well as by the lodging list of mostly high officials that also includes the prophet Quqî (SAA 7 9 r. i 23). One might ask whether the prophecy of Remutti-Allati, spoken "in the middle of the mountains" (SAA 9 1.3), was uttered on the battlefield.

third party are better documented. The best examples are the pertinent letters of Queen Šibtu of Mari[74] and the Assyrian prophecies formally addressed to Naqia, the king's mother (SAA 9 1.7; 1.8; 5).

Female intermediaries, whether at Mari or in Assyria, commonly transmitted words of female prophets. The female-through-female communication was not exclusive, though, since the royal women of Mari—Šibtu, Inib-šina, Addu-duri, and others—report appearances of male persons as well,[75] and male officials, both at Mari and in Assyria, give accounts of female prophets.[76] It is noteworthy, however, that three out of four known personal names of Mari prophetesses are transmitted by female writers,[77] and that both oracles to Naqia in which the name of the prophet is extant are spoken by female prophets.[78] This evidence suggests that the royal women were in closer contact with prophetesses than the male persons of the court. In the case of Naqia, the relationship with the prophetesses may be based on personal contacts with the personnel of Ištar temples, all the more probable since many prophecies and other texts refer to the nursing of the Assyrian princes "in the lap" of the goddess, which probably has a concrete point of reference in entrusting the royal infants to the temples of Ištar.[79]

---

74 ARM 26 207; 208; 211; 212; 213; 214; 236; for the correspondence of Šibtu, see W. H. Ph. Römer, *Frauenbriefe über Religion, Politik und Privatleben in Māri: Untersuchungen zu G. Dossin, Archives Royales de Mari X (Paris, 1967)* (AOAT 12; Kevelaer, Germany: Butzon & Bercker; Neukirchen-Vluyn: Neukirchener, 1971); Pinhas Artzi and Abraham Malamat, "The Correspondence of Šibtu, Queen of Mari in *ARM* X," *Or* 40 (1971): 75–89 (reprinted in Abraham Malamat, *Mari and the Bible* [SHANE 12; Leiden: Brill, 1998], 175–91); Sasson, "Posting," 303–8.

75 Šibtu: ARM 26 208 (Qišti-Diritim); Addu-duri: ARM 26 195 (Iṣi-ahu); 237 (Dadâ); 238 (Iddin-Ili).

76 Mari: ARM 26 201: Bahdi-Lim (*muhhūtum*); ARM 26 210: Kibri-Dagan (*awiltum aššat awīlim*); ARM 26 199: Sammetar (*qammatum*); ARM 26 200: Ahum (Hubatum *muhhūtum*). Assyria: SAA 10 352: Mar-Issar (*raggintu*); SAA 13 37: Adad-ahu-iddina (Mullissu-abu-uṣri *raggintu*); SAA 13 144: Nabû-reši-išši (name unknown, female).

77 I.e., Ahatum the slave girl (ARM 26 214: Šibtu), Kakka-lidi (ARM 26 236: Šibtu), and Innibana the *āpiltum* (ARM 26 204: Inib-šina); only the name of Hubatum the *muhhūtum* is reported by a male writer (ARM 26 200: Ahum). Note also that the names of the *assinnus* Šelebum (ARM 26 197: Inib-šina; 213: Šibtu) and Ilihaznaja (ARM 26 212: Šibtu) are mentioned by women only (the writer of ARM 26 198 is unknown).

78 I.e., SAA 9 1.7 (Issar-beli-daʾʾini) and 1.8 (Ahat-abiša); in SAA 9 5, the name, if indicated, is destroyed. In addition, the king's mother is mentioned in SAA 9 2.1 i 13 and 2.6 iv 28 (?).

79 E.g., SAA 9 7 r. 6: *ša Mullissu ummašūni lā tapallah ša Bēlet Arbail tārīssūni lā*

This only adds to the evidence that the worship of Ištar was the primary setting for the Assyrian prophets' socioreligious role, within which even the connection between the prophets and the king was established. The position of the prophets as servants of the goddess entitled them to communication with the king; on the other hand, it also enabled them to express demands to the king and even to criticize his comportment. Even though, ideologically, there should have been no discrepancy between the king's decisions and the divine will, the king was a human being, liable to commit offenses against the divine world. Hence, the potential for a conflict between the god and the king, forcefully actualized in the biblical prophecy, existed even in Assyria. Esarhaddon, for instance, was explicitly reminded at his coronation of his obligations to Ištar (SAA 9 3.5 iii 18–37). Even though this prophecy deals with cultic matters reminiscent of similar demands in Mari letters[80] and, for example, of Mal 1:11–14, no distinction should be made between "cultic" and "social" criticism, since perfection is required of the king in both respects. The lack of social demands in the extant Neo-Assyrian prophecies[81] does not mean that the social offenses of the king, according to the prevailing standards, were not of concern to the goddess and her servants.

That Neo-Assyrian prophecies have been preserved only from the time of Esarhaddon and Assurbanipal raises the question whether

---

tapallah, "You whose mother is Mullissu, have no fear! You whose nurse is Lady of Arbela, have no fear!"; SAA 3 13 r. 6–8: *ṣehru atta Aššūr-bāni apli ša umušširūka ina muhhi Šarrat Nīnua lakû atta Aššur-bāni-apli ša ašbaku ina burki Šarrat Nīnua,* "You were a child, Assurbanipal, when I left you with the Queen of Nineveh; you were a baby, Assurbanipal, when you sat in the lap of the Queen of Nineveh!" For entrusting the Assyrian princes to temples of Ištar, and for further references, see Parpola, *Assyrian Prophecies,* xxxix–xl; ic–c, nn. 174–77.

80 E.g., ARM 26 215:15–21: *muhhûm pān Dagan [i]tbīma kīʾam iqbi u[m]māmi šūma admati mê zakūtim ul ašatti ana bēlīka šupurma u mê zakūtim lišqenni,* "A prophet arose before Dagan and spoke: 'How long shall I not be able to drink pure water? Write to your lord that he would provide me with pure water!'"

81 The archives of Mari contain traces of such prophetic demands, especially in the letters of Nur-Sîn from Aleppo (A. 1121+ and A. 1968), for which see Sasson, "Posting," 314–16; Jean-Georges Heintz, "Des textes sémitiques anciens à la Bible hébraïque: Un comparatisme légitime?" in *Le comparatisme en histoire des religions* (ed. François Bœspflug and Françoise Dunand; Paris: Cerf, 1997), 127–56, esp. 136–50; Herbert B. Huffmon, "The Expansion of Prophecy in the Mari Archives: New Texts, New Readings, New Information," in *Prophecy and Prophets: The Diversity of Contemporary Issues in Scholarship* (ed. Yehoshua Gitay; SBL Semeia Studies; Atlanta: Scholars Press, 1997), 7–22, esp. 16–17; Malamat, *Mari and the Bible,* 151–56.

these kings were the only ones to promote prophecy, to the extent that their words were not only filed in the archives but also quoted by the scribes who authored their inscriptions.[82] The existing sources indeed give the impression that the activity of prophets, while not restricted to this period, enjoyed a higher social esteem during the reigns of Esarhaddon and Assurbanipal than ever before in Assyria. The extant documents from the time of the previous Sargonid kings include no mention of prophets, nor do documents from earlier periods provide information about prophets' existence, except for a couple of Middle and Neo-Assyrian decrees of expenditures in which prophets are listed among recipients of food rations.[83] If this argument *ex silentio* is consistent with reality, it may be assumed that, while the prophets were there all the time, the kings valued them differently at different times.

However, there is more than one side to the matter. The overwhelming majority of the material in the Assyrian archives derives from the reigns of Esarhaddon and Assurbanipal, while the percentage of sources from the time of earlier Sargonid kings is modest indeed. In fact, the archives of Nineveh and Mari are by far the most abundant Mesopotamian archives, and it may not be a pure coincidence that it is in these two sets of sources that the extant Mesopotamian prophecies are to be found. That these huge archives include just a few prophetic documents from the decades prior to their destruction indicates that, if prophetic reports were written and even stored, they were normally not meant for long-term preservation.[84] Hence, the small quantity of prophecy in the existing sources is not an accurate indicator of the significance of prophecy, any more than the total lack of letters from the time of Sennacherib implies that he had no correspondence.

While the silence of the sources yields only ambiguous interpretations, two arguments in favor of the special appreciation of prophecy

[82] It is conceivable that the prophecies of SAA 9 1 and 3 were used by the author(s) of Esarhaddon's Nin A inscription (see Weippert, "Assyrische Prophetien," 93–95; Parpola, *Assyrian Prophecies*, lxviii–lxi; Nissinen, *References*, 30–31), and at least some of the prophetic quotations in the inscriptions of Assurbanipal may be cited from written sources (see Nissinen, *References*, 58–61).

[83] SAA 12 69; VS 19 1; see above.

[84] Tablets with a single prophetic oracle are attested form Ešnunna (FLP 1674; 2064) and Assyria (SAA 9 7–11), but not from Mari; archival copies of collections of oracles are only known from Assyria. Cf. Nissinen, "Spoken, Written, Quoted, and Invented."

by the kings Esarhaddon and Assurbanipal remain. First, only Esarhaddon apparently had prophecies recopied and compiled in collections, consciously preserving them for posterity. Second, the inscriptions of Tiglath-Pileser III, Sargon II, and Sennacherib in all their comprehensiveness make no mention of prophets. While the Sargonid kings in general—and not only Esarhaddon, traditionally regarded as especially "superstitious"—showed a remarkable interest in omens of different kinds,[85] it is clear that Esarhaddon and Assurbanipal in their inscriptions refer to divination, including prophecy, more than their predecessors. But even under their reigns, the scholars—haruspices, astrologers, exorcists—are better represented in the sources than the prophets.

The Prophets and Other Diviners

It is typical of the Neo-Assyrian royal inscriptions that prophecies (*šipir mahhê*) are mentioned together with other forms of divination. The Nin A inscription of Esarhaddon, calling prophecies "messages of the gods and the goddess" (*našparti ilāni u Ištar;* Nin A ii 6), equates them with "favorable omens in the sky and on earth." In the Ass A inscription, prophecies appear together with astrological omens and dreams, as well as with *egerrû*-oracles (Ass A ii 12–22), which, at least at Mari, are more or less equivalent to prophecies.[86] Likewise, an inscription of Assurbanipal bundles "good omens, dreams, *egerrû*-oracles, and prophetic messages" (B v 95). These lists of divinatory methods are reminiscent not only of 1 Sam 28:6, in which King Saul, before turning to a necromancer, is said to have tried dreams, Urim, and prophets, but also of the Hittite prayers in which the king seeks relief

[85] See F. M. Fales and Giovanni B. Lanfranchi, "The Impact of Oracular Material on the Political Utterances and Political Action in the Royal Inscriptions of the Sargonid Dynasty," in Heintz, *Oracles et prophéties dans l'antiquité*, 99–114. Note also the "anti-divinatory" attitude of one of the editions (E) of Esarhaddon's Babylon inscription; see Mordechai Cogan, "Omens and Ideology in the Babylon Inscription of Esarhaddon," in *History, Historiography, and Interpretation: Studies in Biblical and Cuneiform Literatures* (ed. Hayim Tadmor and Moshe Weinfeld; Jerusalem: Magnes Press; Leiden: Brill, 1983), 76–87.

[86] For *egerrû* at Mari, see ARM 26 196:8–10; 207:4–11; 244:11–14; cf. Durand, *Archives*, 385; Sally A. L. Butler, *Mesopotamian Conceptions of Dreams and Dream Rituals* (AOAT 258; Münster: Ugarit-Verlag, 1998), 151–57.

from plagues by different divinatory means, eventually including prophecy of some kind.[87]

Listing techniques of divination implies that difference among them was acknowledged; even prophecy stands in its own right. However, the means prophets used for receiving divine messages were not exclusively "prophetic," that is, typical of the prophets only. There were ecstatics besides prophets; visions and dreams could be experienced by other people as well; and, in many cases, the difference between prophetic and other noninductive divination, or "possession divination," is extremely difficult to define. On the other hand, the inductive methods of divination required specialized studies and could be practiced only by experts whose methods did not considerably overlap. Astrologers observed celestial phenomena while haruspices interpreted viscera of sacrificial animals, never vice versa. However, their respective expertises were complementary, and scholarly cooperation evidently existed.[88] What united the scholars of different kinds (astrologers, haruspices, and exorcists) was their scholarship, the profound knowledge of traditional literature, and a high level of literacy—qualities that are not prerequisites to noninductive divinatory skills, which may not include literary activity at all.

Hence, if we want to divide divination into subcategories, the basis of division cannot be the difference between prophecy and all other kinds of divination. The dividing lines should be drawn between different techniques of divination; there are also differences between the social roles of the techniques' practitioners. The Assyrian prophets are a class distinct from the scholars, differing in gender, social standing and politics.

---

87 See Oliver R. Gurney, "Hittite Prayers of Mursili II," *AAA* 27 (1940): 26–27 (*KUB* 24 3 ii 19–22 = *KUB* 24 4 i 10–12); Albrecht Goetze, *Die Pestgebete des Muršiliš* (Kleinasiatische Forschungen 1; Weimar, 1927–1930), 218–19 (Pestgebet 2 §10); and cf. Annelies Kammenhuber, *Orakelpraxis, Träume und Vorzeichenschau bei den Hethitern* (Hethitische Texte 7; Heidelberg: Winter, 1976), 119–33; Manfred Weippert, "Aspekte israelitischer Prophetie im Lichte verwandter Erscheinungen des Alten Orients," in *Ad bene et fideliter seminandum: Festgabe für Karlheinz Deller* (ed. Gerlinde Mauer and Ursula Magen; AOAT 220; Kevelaer, Germany: Butzon & Bercker; Neukirchen-Vluyn: Neukirchener, 1988), 287–319, esp. 297–99.

88 See Simo Parpola, "Mesopotamian Astrology and Astronomy as Domains of the Mesopotamian 'Wisdom,'" in *Die Rolle der Astronomie in den Kulturen Mesopotamiens* (ed. Hannes D. Galter; Grazer Morgenländische Studien 3; Graz, Austria: Universitätsbibliothek, 1993), 47–59, esp. 51–52.

First, the majority of the Assyrian prophets known to us are women, while there is no female representative among the scholars.

Second, as noted earlier, prophets, unlike scholars, do not write letters to the king; if their words are written, they are transmitted to the king in reports written by professional scribes.[89]

Third, while scholars transmitted received tradition as successors of the mythical, antediluvian sages,[90] prophets acted as direct mouthpieces of gods; both roles were the result of education and training in a specific environment.

Fourth, prophets do not take part in political counseling in the way of the scholars; they do not form part of the king's closest advisory body and were not members of the political elite, or the "magnates" (LÚ.GAL.MEŠ).[91] This does not prevent them, by the medium of oracles, from being actively involved in political decision making, but unlike the scholars they do not seem to be in the position of making practical suggestions. Scholars sometimes make suggestions on the grounds of prophetic oracles,[92] but more often on the basis of their learned observations and political instinct.

In Assyria, the roles of scholar and prophet are not interchangeable. The inductive and noninductive methods of divination are never mixed, although, in a literary context, the outcome of divination may sometimes be described in a way that resembles prophecy.[93] However, when dreams and visions are reported, for example, in inscriptions, the source seems immaterial to the author, and it is often impossible to decide whether the dream or vision in question should be defined

---

89 See Nissinen, "Spoken, Written, Quoted, and Invented."

90 See Simo Parpola, *Letters from Assyrian and Babylonian Scholars* (SAA 10; Helsinki: Helsinki University Press, 1993), xvii–xxiv.

91 For the officials belonging to this class, see Raija Mattila, *The King's Magnates: A Study of the Highest Officials of the Neo-Assyrian Empire* (SAAS 11; Helsinki: Neo-Assyrian Text Corpus Project, 2000); Simo Parpola, "The Assyrian Cabinet," in *Vom Alten Orient zum Alten Testament: Festschrift für Wolfram von Soden* (ed. Manfried Dietrich and Oswald Loretz; AOAT 240; Kevelaer, Germany: Butzon & Bercker; Neukirchen-Vluyn: Neukirchener, 1995), 379–401.

92 As Bel-ušezib does in SAA 10 111 and Nabû-nadin-šumi in SAA 10 284; see Nissinen, *References*, 96–105.

93 E.g., Esarhaddon Nin A i 61–62: *alik lā kalâta idāka nittallakma ninâra gārēka,* "Go ahead, do not hold back! We walk by your side, we annihilate your enemies!" These words are called *šīr takilti,* "oracle of encouragement," which refers to extispicy; see Nissinen, *References*, 33–34; Pongratz-Leisten, *Herrschaftswissen*, 84–85.

as prophetic.[94] Visionaries like the *šabrû* and the *šāʾilu* are virtually equated with prophets in Neo-Assyrian texts, and the dreams of *šabrûs* recorded in the prisms of Assurbanipal are reported in language that could also be used by the Assyrian prophets.

What makes the prophets distinctive from others in Neo-Assyrian society is their attachment to the worship of Ištar and to the respective socioreligious role, comparable to that of other devotees like the *assinnu* and *kurgarrû,* whose gender role was permanently changed by the goddess. The prophets may not have been generally characterized by a specific gender role, although indications to that effect exist (see above); in any case, the association of *mahhû* and *raggimu* with other ecstatics and the connotation of frantic behavior suggest that to be a prophet required a role and way of life distinctive from that of an average Assyrian citizen. Like the representatives of the "third gender," the prophets impersonated the goddess—at least functionally, if not in their outer appearance. This explains the prominent role of women in prophecy without making it solely an *affaire de femmes:* the goddess who is able to take the role of both sexes can be impersonated by female and male persons alike.

All this is not to say that the purpose of prophecy would have been different from that of divination in general. The difference is qualitative rather than functional; all branches of divination share a common ideological and theological basis. In Assyrian imperial ideology, there should not have been any discrepancy among prophets, scholars, and other diviners who worked for a common goal, for example, during the war of Esarhaddon against his brothers.[95] The legitimation of all divination was based on the idea that gods indeed communicate with humans and that the decisions of the heavenly world affect earthly cir-

---

94 For a similar situation at Mari, see Sasson, "Posting," 300. Many Mari letters conventionally included in the "prophetic" corpus are, in fact, dream reports (e.g., ARM 26 233; 234; 235; 236; 238; 239; 240; and other letters classified under the title "Les rêves" in Durand, *Archives,* 465–82), and it is often difficult to decide whether they should be qualified as prophetic dreams, if the dreamer her/himself is not designated explicitly as a prophet; for an attempt to differentiate between prophecies and (nonprophetic) dreams in Mari letters, see Ichiro Nakata, "Two Remarks on the So-Called Prophetic Texts from Mari," *Acta Sumerologica* 4 (1982): 143–48. As to Mari dreams in general, see Jack M. Sasson, "Mari Dreams," *JAOS* 103 (1983): 283–93; Pongratz-Leisten, *Herrschaftswissen,* 107–11.

95 SAA 9 1.8 and SAA 10 109:8–15 show that the queen mother Naqia consulted prophets (Ahat-abiša) as well as scholars (Bel-ušezib and probably the exorcist Dadâ) during the expatriation of Esarhaddon.

cumstances. There were different channels, however, through which the divine will was brought to humans' attention, as well as different human beings who were qualified to take care of the logistics.

Conclusions

Given the state of publication up to 1998, it is understandable that Neo-Assyrian prophetic documents have not hitherto had a decisive role in the study of prophecy, even though their value to comparative studies has often been acknowledged.[96] Now, having the extant documentation published in an easily accessible form, the time is ripe for a full-scale assessment of the implications of the Neo-Assyrian sources for the understanding of prophecy, both in Mesopotamia[97] and in general; in this essay, this work has been attempted from the point of view of the socioreligious role of the Assyrian prophets.

The Neo-Assyrian sources we have at our disposal—both the actual prophetic oracles and other texts—make prophets appear as practitioners of one branch of noninductive divination, whose characteristic role as devotees of Ištar also brought them into a close relationship with the king. Apart from the Neo-Assyrian sources, prophetic oracles and documents concerning the appearance of prophets (*mahhû/muhhûm*) show, in all their sparsity, that prophecy in Mesopotamia was not just an accidental and temporary phenomenon, imported from somewhere else in the Neo-Assyrian era, but that prophets were there all the time. If the worship of Ištar may be claimed as "genuinely" Mesopotamian, this claim certainly applies to prophecy.

Regarding the Assyrian prophets' socioreligious role and its implications for the image of the prophet in the ancient Near East, the Neo-Assyrian sources reinforce the elementary connection of prophecy with temples and the royal court, known from the sources from Mari

96 Apart from the few works by Herbert B. Huffmon, Manfred Weippert, and others dedicated to the Neo-Assyrian prophetic sources (see the bibliography, including works dated before 1997, in Parpola, *Assyrian Prophecies*, cix–cxii), see, e.g., Robert R. Wilson, *Prophecy and Society in Ancient Israel* (Philadelphia: Fortress Press, 1980), 111–19; José Luis Sicre, *Profetismo en Israel: El profeta, los profetas, el mensaje* (Estella, Spain: Verbo divino, 1992), 238–40; Lester L. Grabbe, *Priests, Prophets, Diviners, Sages: A Socio-historical Study of Religious Specialists in Ancient Israel* (Valley Forge, Pa.: Trinity Press International, 1995), 91–92.

97 For a fresh and comprehensive treatment of the Mesopotamian oracular sources, including the prophetic sources, see Pongratz-Leisten, *Herrschaftswissen*, 47–95 (for Assyrian sources, esp. 74–95).

and Ešnunna, as well as from the Hebrew Bible. However, the image of the Assyrian prophet sketched above turns out to be different from the widespread idea of prophecy, based largely on biblical material and interpreted within the symbolic world of modern scholarship; the following presentation of the prophet's image, as opposed to the image of the priest, appeared in a recent reconstruction of ancient Israelite society:

> Prophets claim to have been individually called by a deity, that is, their vocation is customarily not inherited or taught, as is the case for priests. Prophets tend not to be associated with institutions. And prophets are less concerned than priests with maintaining the status quo; that is, they are usually more involved in promoting dynamic social change as innovators and reformers.[98]

This hardly matches the picture of the prophets of Mari or Assyria, who were associated with institutions, in the framework of which their expertise was taught and learned, and who—at least on the basis of the extant sources—were apparently not the first to promote social change. If there were prophets like those described above, no documentation of their activity has been preserved. Moreover, the idea of prophecy as quoted is problematic even in view of the Hebrew Bible. The idea of antagonism between the prophet and the priest may be wrong—Jeremiah, for example, is introduced as *min hak-kōhănîm,* that is, a priest (Jer 1:1).[99] Furthermore, the Hebrew Bible is explicit about associating the prophets with the temple of Jerusalem or other cult places, even in cases in which the prophet takes a critical attitude toward the official cult. For example, the biblical figures of Jeremiah or Ezekiel are unthinkable without the temple of Jerusalem in the background, not to mention Haggai and Zechariah and their ultimatums

---

[98] Paula McNutt, *Reconstructing the Society of Ancient Israel* (Library of Ancient Israel; London: SPCK; Louisville: Westminster John Knox Press, 1999), 179. Note that the author herself also acknowledges different types of prophets: "Presumably, prophets who upheld the status quo (and thus were not associated with types of movements described here) would have been supported by those in power, and peripheral prophets, who were critical of the status quo, by those who wanted some kind of a change" (180–81).

[99] See, e.g., Robert P. Carroll, *The Book of Jeremiah: A Commentary* (OTL; London: SCM, 1986), 90–91. Even if *min hak-kōhănîm* should be understood as a reference to Jeremiah's father Hilkiah and not to himself (thus William McKane, *A Critical and Exegetical Commentary on Jeremiah* [vol. 1; ICC; Edinburgh: T. & T. Clark, 1986], 1), it does not change the socioreligious background of Jeremiah as being from priestly circles.

on reconstruction of the Second Temple. There are innovators, reformers, and promoters of dynamic social change among the biblical prophets, but one might ask about the breadth of evidence for this kind of prophecy and to what extent it goes back to historical circumstances. In other words, to what extent does "biblical prophecy"—prophecy as depicted in the final form of the Hebrew Bible—correspond to "ancient Israelite prophecy," the concrete historical phenomenon? The prophetic literature of the Hebrew Bible is the result of centuries of selecting, editing, and interpreting, and can give only a partial and somewhat distorted view of the phenomenon.[100] It is widely accepted today that the biblical prophetic figures represent an amalgamation of subsequent generations' interpretations,[101] behind and among which the historical figures of the prophets must be sought—if there is a methodology, or methodologies, that enable this quest.

While it may be a hopeless task to reconstruct historical personalities from the biblical prophetic texts—even redaction criticism can only identify strands of material, from different ages, that remain ultimately anonymous—comparative studies are helpful in outlining ancient Israelite prophecy and the roles of the prophets, provided that each source is studied in its own right and hasty conclusions are avoided.[102] From the comparative point of view, the Neo-Assyrian prophetic sources are no doubt prominent: not only do they derive

---

100 See Grabbe, *Priests, Prophets, Diviners, Sages*, 117: "The impression is frequently given that the OT prophets were primarily social critics and ethicists. This is based partly on a failure to consider the contents of the prophetic books as a whole and partly on a failure to recognize that the contents of prophetic books are not necessarily the product of prophets. That is, in the course of transmission and editing of the tradition, the contents of the prophetic books may well be to a significant extent the product of scribes, priests, and sages."

101 For Jeremiah, see Carroll, *Jeremiah*, 55–64; for Ezekiel, see Karl-Friedrich Pohlmann, *Das Buch des Propheten Hesekiel (Ezechiel): Kapitel 1–19* (ATD 22/1; Göttingen: Vandenhoeck & Ruprecht, 1996), 40–41; for Amos, see Christoph Levin, "Das Amosbuch der Anawim," *ZTK* 94 (1997): 407–36; for the problem in general, see, e.g., Odil Hannes Steck, *Die Prophetenbücher und ihr theologisches Zeugnis: Wege der Nachfrage und Fährten zur Antwort* (Tübingen: Mohr, 1996).

102 For comparative attempts of different kinds, see, e.g., Oswald Loretz, "Die Entstehung des Amos-Buches im Licht der Prophetien aus Māri, Assur, Ishchali und der Ugarit-Texte: Paradigmenwechsel in der Prophetenforschung," *UF* 24 (1992): 179–215; Hans M. Barstad, "No Prophets? Recent Developments in Biblical Prophetic Research and Ancient Near Eastern Prophecy," *JSOT* 57 (1993): 39–60 (reprinted in *The Prophets: A Sheffield Reader* [ed. Philip R. Davies; Biblical

from the height of Assyrian political and cultural influence, acknowledged as a key period in the literary and ideological formation of the Hebrew Bible,[103] they also demonstrate textual, metaphorical, and ideological affinities with prophetic and other biblical texts.[104] These texts, together with similar texts in other ancient Near Eastern prophetic sources, make interpretation of ancient Israelite/Judean prophecy as an indigenous phenomenon unwarranted.[105] While it is unsound methodology to maintain that conclusions from the Assyrian evidence apply to ancient Israelite society, so that the image of the Israelite/Judean prophets could be drawn from the Assyrian model,[106] it is also true that Neo-Assyrian prophetic sources provide, chronologically, the most immediate point of comparison for the biblical prophetic literature. They also provide the closest historical and phenomenological analogy to ancient Israelite/Judean prophecy.

Seminar 42; Sheffield: Sheffield Academic Press, 1996], 106–26); Heintz, "Des textes sémitiques anciens à la Bible hébraïque." On the comparative approach, see also the contributions of Hans M. Barstad and Lester L. Grabbe in this volume.

103 See, e.g., Eckart Otto, "Die besiegten Sieger: Von der Macht und Ohnmacht der Ideen in der Geschichte am Beispiel der neuassyrischen Großreichspolitik," *BZ* 43 (1999): 180–203.

104 See Weippert, "Assyrische Prophetien," 104–11; Nissinen, "Relevanz," 225–53; Parpola, *Assyrian Prophecies,* passim.

105 *Pace* Robert R. Wilson, "Prophet," *HBD* 884–89, esp. 886: "[T]here is no biblical evidence to indicate that Israel recognized prophecy as an import. In addition, anthropological studies of prophetic phenomena show that prophecy can arise spontaneously in any society when the necessary social and religious conditions are present. There is therefore no reason to assume that prophets could not have appeared in Israel without outside cultural influence." While the chronological and geographical distribution of ancient Near Eastern prophecy raises the question whether prophecy anywhere in the ancient Near East can be considered a foreign import, it also speaks for prophecy's cultural communicability rather than for unique and isolated phenomena.

106 See the just warnings of Joseph Blenkinsopp, *Sage, Priest, Prophet: Religious and Intellectual Leadership in Ancient Israel* (Library of Ancient Israel; Louisville: Westminster John Knox Press, 1995), 6–7.

7

Arabian Prophecy

Jaakko Hämeen-Anttila

Studies on Arabian prophecy have not progressed much in the last few decades. Standard textbooks give detailed information on Muḥammad, the Prophet of Islam, as described in traditional sources, and mention briefly the soothsayers—the *kāhins*—and their modern, mainly South Arabian, parallels. In addition, the so-called *ridda* prophets[1] are sometimes mentioned in connection with Muḥammad's life or the early development of the Islamic state. Yet the recent development in early Islamic studies necessitates a reevaluation of the question of prophecy. The traditional view of early Arabian prophecy has been drawn mainly from Muslim sources, which have been taken to reflect more or less exactly the pre-Islamic and early Islamic history.[2] Recent studies on early Islamic history have shown that this is not the case. The written material, with the notable exception of the Qurʾān, rarely dates from before 800 C.E., and even then cannot be followed more than a few decades backward.[3] The sources alleging to describe the late-sixth- to early-seventh-century Arabian Peninsula tell us, in fact, more about the late-eighth-century prejudices of their Syrian and

[1] To distinguish between the canonized Islamic prophets—Muḥammad and his predecessors—and Arabian prophets in the margins of Islam and contemporary with, or slightly later than, Muḥammad, I use the term "*ridda* prophets" (for the term *ridda*, see below, n. 72). I do not imply that other prophets were much different from Muḥammad. In scholarly literature, they are often simply called pseudoprophets.

[2] In the nineteenth century, a line of study discussed the Arabian *kāhins* in connection with Semitic prophecy and sacerdotal office, the last monument of which is, in a sense, Toufic Fahd, *La divination arabe: Études religieuses, sociologiques et folkloriques sur le milieu natif de l'Islam* (Leiden: Brill, 1966). While doing much groundbreaking work, these scholars made the mistake of reading the Arabic material in the light of Semitic parallels and then using it to prove the existence of religious institutions in the Common Semitic period.

[3] Some scholars accept the traditional view of the oral tradition's reliability, the so-called *ḥadīth* material, but this view has become more difficult to defend the more our understanding of early Islam has advanced.

Mesopotamian authors than about pre-Islamic times. At the same time it has been realized that the image given in the biography of Muḥammad (*Sirah*) is a hagiography, molded in the late eighth century to fit the paradigm of Jewish and Christian prophets and holy men.

The early development of Islam, until the consolidation of Sunnism in the ninth century and Shiism in the tenth, is also in need of reevaluation. To take but one example: the finality of Muḥammad's prophethood, his place as the Seal of the Prophets (*khātam al-anbiyāʾ*; Qur. 33:40), has lately been seen in a new light.[4] The doctrine did not emerge in his own time, but was formulated only later. For his contemporary followers, Muḥammad was the Seal that confirmed the message of the earlier prophets, not the final Seal that ended the procession of biblical[5] prophets universally. The term "prophet" (*nabī*) may later have been avoided, but the idea of continuous prophecy existed in sectarian Islam. Would-be prophets appeared especially until the ninth century, and new divinely inspired books were written throughout the centuries (e.g., *Umm al-Kitāb* and *Kitāb al-Haft waʾl-aẓilla* in the ninth century,[6] and the books of Bāb in the nineteenth).

There is ample reason to take a fresh look at Arabian prophecy, from the sixth century until the consolidation of Islam around 800 C.E., both for its own sake and for comparative reasons. After all, the study of West Semitic prophecy, attested in Mari, Assyria, and Israel, may profit from South Semitic comparative material, despite the later date for the latter.

---

[4] See Gedaliahu G. Stroumsa, "'Seal of the Prophets': The Nature of a Manichaean Metaphor," *Jerusalem Studies in Arabic and Islam* 7 (1986): 61–74, and Yohanan Friedmann, "Finality of Prophethood in Sunnī Islām," *Jerusalem Studies in Arabic and Islam* 7 (1986): 177–215.

[5] In Islamic studies, "biblical" refers to the Jewish and Christian tradition in general, thus also including the extracanonical material. The word "biblical" is used in this wide sense ("belonging to the Jewish and/or Christian tradition") in this essay. From an Islamic point of view, the legends concerning Moses or Jesus are biblical, even if they are not attested in the Bible itself.

[6] For these two, see Heinz Halm, *Die islamische Gnosis: Die extreme Schia und die ʿAlawiten* (Zürich and Munich: Artemis 1982); for the books of Bāb, see Peter Smith, *The Babi and Baha'i Religions: From Messianic Shi'ism to a World Religion* (Cambridge: Cambridge University Press, 1987). I have studied the oldest part of the *Umm al-Kitāb,* the so-called Jābir Apocalypse (Jaakko Hämeen-Anttila, "Descent and Ascent in Islamic Myth," in *Myths and Mythologies* [ed. Simo Parpola and Robert M. Whiting; Melammu 2; forthcoming]), from the point of view of the descent and ascent myths.

Historiography in Islamic Studies

It is necessary to update the historiographical situation in early Islamic studies.[7] Since 1977, it has become more evident to scholars in the field that the Islamic source material can only be used with great caution—according to the most radical scholars, it may not be used at all, but this extreme fastidiousness, because of its agnostic attitude, has not proven fruitful.[8] The Islamic historical texts all date from the late eighth century or later and have undergone "harmonization" When, in the ninth century, Sunni Islam reached its classical form, the origins of the community were rewritten and all earlier, mainly oral, material had to be harmonized with the classical view of Islam. Only the Qurʾān dates to the early seventh century.[9] The descriptions of pre-Islamic society in classical sources are also questionable, for two reasons. First, the main motive for writing pre-Islamic history was to create a contrast

---

[7] For recent theoretical attempts to cope with early history, the following works may be consulted: Patricia Crone and Michael Cook, *Hagarism: The Making of the Islamic World* (Cambridge: Cambridge University Press, 1977), the ultrarevisionist book which started a tempestuous discussion that continues; Albrecht Noth and Lawrence I. Conrad, *The Early Arabic Historical Tradition: A Source-Critical Study* (Studies in Late Antiquity and Early Islam 3; Princeton, N.J.: Darwin Press, 1994), the rewritten form of Noth's classic study which provided, in its German original (1973), the methodological starting point for all revisionist studies; R. Stephen Humphreys, *Islamic History: A Framework for Inquiry* (Princeton: Princeton University Press, 1991); Chase F. Robinson, "The Study of Islamic Historiography: A Progress Report," *JRAS* (3d ser.) 7/2 (1997): 199–227; and Fred McGraw Donner, *Narratives of Islamic Origins: The Beginnings of Islamic Historical Writing* (Studies in Late Antiquity and Early Islam 14; Princeton, N.J.: Darwin Press, 1998). The latter three are mildly conservative but very sober. See also Tarif Khalidi, *Arabic Historical Thought in the Classical Period* (Cambridge Studies in Islamic Civilization; Cambridge: Cambridge University Press, 1994), a conservative study that is sometimes inaccurate; Wilfred Madelung, *The Succession to Muḥammad: A Study of the Early Caliphate* (Cambridge: Cambridge University Press, 1997), an ultraconservative book from a well-known specialist (see, e.g., my review in *AcOr* 58 [1997]: 215–20).

[8] Crone and Cook, *Hagarism*, and John Wansbrough, *Quranic Studies: Sources and Methods of Scriptural Interpretation* (London Oriental Series 31; Oxford: Oxford University Press, 1977), are good examples of the fruitless attempt to ignore classical source material.

[9] Wansbrough, *Quranic Studies*, sees the Qurʾān as the result of a lengthy oral tradition and the work of several local prophets. Even though Wansbrough's thesis would fit my view of early Arabian prophecy, there is not much evidence to support a late date for the Qurʾān. Wansbrough's basic mistake is to use biblical methods blindly: he starts with the assumption that the Qurʾān was compiled in the same way as several books of the Old Testament and uses OT methods accordingly, without asking himself whether the methods are applicable.

to Islam. Second, in many cases, the less tendentious writers described the bedouin society of their own time and retrojected it to the past.

Islam had been born on the Arabian Peninsula in the early seventh century, but the religion was still in its infancy when, during the conquests, it came to the old cultural area of the Near East. Theological structures, except for a strict monotheism, were still lacking, and the sacred geography[10] and *Heilsgeschichte* were very much in preliminary form. In this situation, the nascent religion, which was too young to be called "Islam"—a term the believers did not use[11]—was heavily influenced by the cognate religions. Extensive contacts were made in Iraq, Syria, and Palestine, although the role of Egypt remained marginal for reasons not yet fully understood.

During the seventh and eighth centuries, the new religion emerged little by little as Islam, by absorbing Jewish, Christian, gnostic,[12] and perhaps other influences; different sects were born during the process. The biography of the prophet Muḥammad was fixed at about the same time, at the end of the eighth century. It was written to fit him into the paradigm of Near Eastern prophets and holy men but also to support the leading role the caliph had taken in the late seventh century.[13] To put it briefly, Muḥammad had to become a kind of victorious Jesus. His character had to absorb the features of a Jewish/Christian prophet who had been denied by his people, but also

---

10 Mekka became overwhelmingly important only around 700 C.E., when it was finally fixed as the Holy City of Islam. Before that, Jerusalem had successfully competed for the position of the first city of Islam.

11 This point has been emphasized by Donner, *Narratives.*

12 I use the term "gnostic" in a broad sense, to mean ideologies and religious concepts influenced by and cognate to gnosticism. For the recent discussion of the term "gnosticism," see, e.g., Michael Allen Williams, *Rethinking "Gnosticism": An Argument for Dismantling a Dubious Category* (Princeton: Princeton University Press, 1996), which perhaps goes too far in its purism. Mandaeans, Manichaeans, and Harranians are among the "gnostic" sects which we know still existed in the Near East and could have influenced some forms of Islam.

13 The now-classic study of the early Islamic caliphate is Patricia Crone and Martin Hinds, *God's Caliph: Religious Authority in the First Centuries of Islam* (University of Cambridge Oriental Publications 37; Cambridge: University of Cambridge Press, 1986). While the two authors are on the right track, I disagree with them when it comes to the profile of the institution directly after the death of Muḥammad. The high spiritual authority of the caliph was, I believe, first claimed by ʿAbdalmalik (d. 705), who also introduced the term "caliph" (*khalīfa*) in the sense of the ruler of the community and its spiritual head—the older, less religiously tinged term for the ruler being *amīr al-muʾminīn,* "the Prince of the Believers."

the features of a ruler and a conqueror, the role model of the caliphs. Yet the harmonization of the sources did not wipe out all memories of the early history of the Arabs; it only buried them under other materials, and the digging for the possibly genuine material is a task which has only just begun.[14]

Traditions of Arabian Prophecy

Prophecy had a long tradition on the peninsula, leading far back beyond the birth of Muḥammad—whether up to the Common Semitic period or not is a question which can probably never be answered adequately. In any case, the Qurʾān itself testifies to the existence of Arab prophets (Hūd, Ṣāliḥ)[15] before Muḥammad, and although the characters themselves are now legendary, it should not make us blind to the fact that both Muḥammad and his audience accepted the idea of earlier, nonbiblical prophets on the peninsula. These prophets were worthy of being Muḥammad's precursors, which, incidentally, shows that they were not considered mere soothsayers. The Qurʾān could speak of Hūd and Ṣāliḥ, two Arab prophets, because the audience accepted them, and the fragmentary narrative implies that the audience knew the rest. The Qurʾān spoke about religious figures familiar to the audience and respected by them.

The interest in a succession of prophets, however, was generated only by the self-identification of Muḥammad with the biblical prophets. Hūd and Ṣāliḥ, like their biblical counterparts, are missing from the earliest parts of the Qurʾān,[16] but when they later did appear, they

---

14 The most remarkable start has been the series Studies in Late Antiquity and Early Islam, in which several important studies have taken earnestly the challenge of the new historiography.

15 There is a South Arabian cult of Hūd, which has been described by R. B. Serjeant ("Hūd and Other Pre-Islamic Prophets," *Le Muséon* 67 [1954]: 121–79, reprinted as no. 1 in R. B. Serjeant, *Studies in Arabian History and Civilisation* [London: Variorum Reprints, 1981]). Despite its title, the article does not, in fact, deal with pre-Islamic times. Other possibly pre-Islamic prophets are mentioned in Friedmann, "Finality," 193–94.

16 Dating the qurʾānic material is still difficult; the best overall system remains that of Theodor Nöldeke, *Geschichte des Qorāns* (ed. Friedrich Schwally, Gotthelf Bergsträsser, and Otto Pretzlvols; vols. 1–3; 2d ed.; Leipzig: Dieterich'sche Verlagsbuchhandlung, 1909–1938). The defect of this system is that it deals with the surahs as wholes and does not take into full account the complexity of the surahs themselves.

were effortlessly accepted into the Islamic holy history. Whether Hūd and Ṣāliḥ might have been biblically inspired prophets or transmitters of a Common Semitic tradition remains open. We cannot rule out the possibility that they had originally been common soothsayers, *kāhins*, who for some reason had been accepted as prophets; the boundary between a *kāhin* and a prophet is very fluid.[17]

In the Qurʾān, Hūd and Ṣāliḥ are mere dummies, who transmit the same message as Muḥammad and all qurʾānic prophets from Abraham to Jesus. The folklore around them, which has been partly written to explain the qurʾānic material, dates considerably later than the Qurʾān and has been generated by the need to get more material into the stories; we have no reason to believe that the stories about Hūd and Ṣāliḥ date to the early seventh century.[18] Thus, all we can say about them is that they—or their models—most probably existed.

The existence of an Arab tradition of prophets is also indirectly supported by the career of Muḥammad himself. As the oldest parts of the Qurʾān show,[19] the original message of Muḥammad was not biblically inspired, yet he was readily accepted by his audience as an inspired man—even those who seem to have opposed him did not find it difficult to accept him as a *kāhin*, *shāʿir*, or *majnūn*, all terms that imply supernatural inspiration.[20] To obey him was more difficult. Thus there was a paradigm into which his earliest audience set Muḥammad. The cornerstone of this paradigm was most probably the *kāhin* (and his female counterpart, the *kāhina*), who received his knowledge from a familiar spirit, *tābiʿ*.[21] *Kāhin*s are found throughout the peninsula and

---

[17] A similar increase in respect is seen in the legends surrounding Saṭīḥ; see below.

[18] The study of Serjeant ("Hūd"), like, in fact, most of his other studies on early Islam, suffers from his ready acceptance of the nineteenth- and twentieth-century South Arabian situation as a replica of pre-Islamic times.

[19] There is an almost complete lack of biblical material in the surahs of the first Mekkan period, if we exclude verses that are obviously later additions.

[20] The Qurʾān (e.g., 52:29; 69:41–42) denies these identifications. Neither *shāʿir* nor *majnūn* is to be understood in their modern sense ("poet"; "madman") but in a more archaic one. The *shāʿir* receives his knowledge from his *tābiʿ*, "familiar spirit," like the *kāhin*, and the *majnūn* is "covered" (which is the literal meaning of the word) by a supernatural being. Ignaz Goldziher, *Abhandlungen zur arabischen Philologie* (Leiden: Brill, 1896), 1:1–105, is a somewhat dated but still-valuable study on the pre-Islamic poet and his inspiration.

[21] The institution of *kihāna* has been studied by Fahd, *Divination*, 92–102; his article *"kāhin"* in the *Encyclopaedia of Islam* (2d ed.; vol. 4; Leiden: Brill, 1978), sum-

may well continue an old Semitic tradition with little, if any, biblical influence. The term *kāhin* is hardly a Hebrew loan (*kōhēn*), and the *kāhin* had few similarities with the Jewish *kōhēn*. These soothsayers seem usually to have restricted their message to the ephemeral, answering questions concerning disagreements, lost camels, or whatever. What they lacked was a universal or, at least, a more general dimension. After the disagreement was settled or the camels found, the *kāhin*'s dicta did not retain much interest and were soon forgotten.

Later Arabic literature tells a lot about these *kāhins*, but the sources are not very reliable. In the biography of the prophet Muḥammad, the *kāhins* are mainly used in the annunciation passages; to collect the greatest possible authority for Muḥammad, each religious authority was used. *Kāhins*, rabbis, and Christian holy men are found testifying to the coming of the new prophet.[22] A well-known case of annunciation through *kāhins* is the story about Shiqq and Saṭīḥ in the court of the South Arabian king Rabīʿa ibn Naṣr, related on the first pages of Muḥammad's biography as it now stands.[23] According to this story, the king sent for these two *kāhins* so that they could explain his dream. Without telling them about it, he asked them to explain the dream in order to prove their clairvoyance. As will be seen, this is a modification of the "*kāhin* test." Both were able to interpret the dream as referring to the country's destiny. When the king questioned them further, they

---

marizes his own monograph. The monograph is useful as a collection of materials, but it does not take the tangled question of source criticism sufficiently into account. What Fahd in fact describes is how later Islamic authors saw the *kihāna*, not what the *kihāna* was before Islam. Stories about *kāhins* appear everywhere in classical Arabic literature. A selection of these stories appears in an-Nuwayrī's (d. 1332) *Nihāya al-arab fī funūn al-adab* (Cairo: Wizārat ath-thaqāfa wa'l-irshād al-qawmī, n.d.), 3:128–34.

[22] See Uri Rubin, *The Eye of the Beholder: The Life of Muḥammad as Viewed by the Early Muslims, a Textual Analysis* (Studies in Late Antiquity and Early Islam 5; Princeton, N.J.: Darwin Press, 1995), 44–55. I have studied part of this material in "The Corruption of Christianity: Salmān al-Fārisī's Quest as a Paradigmatic Model" (StudOr; forthcoming). In Islamic theory, the coming of the new—and final, as he later was defined—prophet ended the age of *kihāna*. Until then, the familiar spirits, or *shayṭāns*, of the *kāhins* had been able to eavesdrop in the lowest heaven, but some time before the call of Muḥammad, these were driven away by shooting stars in order to keep the divine message unblemished by *kihāna*. See, e.g., an-Nuwayrī, *Nihāya*, 3:128, and Qur. 72:1–15.

[23] Ibn Hishām, *as-Sīra an-nabawīya* (ed. Jamāl Thābit, Muḥammad Maḥmūd, and Sayyid Ibrāhīm; vols. 1–5; Cairo: Dār al-ḥadīth, 1996), 1:30–33; A. Guillaume, trans., *The Life of Muhammad: A Translation of Ibn Ishaq's Sirat Rasul Allah* (Oxford:

told briefly about the coming of the new prophet whose nation's dominion would last to the last day.

Already here, we find the theme of Saṭīḥ (as well as Shiqq) prophesying the future. Saṭīḥ, in sources, was traditionally from Syria, and he was also described as prophesying the future conquests of Islam to the king of Persia.[24] The same theme was later developed further, and in Ibn al-Munādī's (d. 947) *Malāḥim* 48–58,[25] Saṭīḥ prophesies the future of the Islamic Empire up to the early tenth century in what we might call the Saṭīḥ Apocalypse. The text is obviously a literary fiction of the tenth century and falls outside the scope of this essay. The Saṭīḥ Apocalypse does, however, testify to the growing interest in the legendary *kāhin*, and this interest seems to have started developing early, although Saṭīḥ is not mentioned in the Qurʾān. In a sense, Saṭīḥ became the role model for *kāhins*. In discussing the *ridda* prophetess Sajāḥi, al-Masʿūdī (d. 956) claims that she had modeled her career after Saṭīḥ before she started prophesying (*Murūj* §1522).[26] At the same time, this text shows that the classical authors saw a difference between a *kāhin* and a *ridda* prophet. These stories of "high prophecy," situated in the courts of the mighty, are connected with the annunciation of the new prophet; their evidential value for the historical *kihāna*, the profession of *kāhin*, is minimal. The more down-to-earth stories of *kāhins* are found in other contexts.

Most of the stories concerning the "low prophecy" of *kāhins* show one and the same structure. A group of clients, or sometimes a single client, comes to the *kāhin*. Before arriving, the client hides something, for example, in one story a dog called Sawwār with an unusual necklace.[27] When the *kāhin* describes the hidden object correctly, he has passed the test of clairvoyance. The client proceeds with his real business, about which he receives the *kāhin*'s response, and the *kāhin* gets

---

Oxford University Press, 1955; repr., Karachi, Pakistan: Oxford University Press, 1982), 4–6. The *Sirah,* using this example, is cited as *Sirah* 1:30–33/4–6, where the numbers before the slash refer to the edition and those after to the translation of Guillaume.

24 An-Nuwayrī, *Nihāya,* 3:128–30.

25 Ibn al-Munādī, *al-Malāḥim* (1418; ed. ʿAbdalkarīm al-ʿUqaylī; Qumm al-muqaddasa: Dār as-Sīra, 1998).

26 Al-Masʿūdī, *Murūj adh-dhahab wa-maʿādin al-jawhar* (ed. Charles Pellat; vols. 1–7; Publications de l'Université Libanaise, Section des études historiques 11; Beirut, 1966–1979).

27 See an-Nuwayrī, *Nihāya,* 3:133.

paid. The *kāhin* never uses accessories (e.g., arrows), but receives his oracle through inspiration.

In the classical sources, the *kāhin* dicta, which can hardly ever be considered authentic but which show what near-contemporaries thought historical, are oracles clothed in obscure phrasing. The language used is *saj*ʿ, rhymed prose, which resembles the language of the oldest parts of the Qurʾān.[28] Many of these *kāhins* seem to have been local prophets or soothsayers. The old sources are more or less unanimous in that they describe people traveling to visit the *kāhin* but never, or rarely, the *kāhin* traveling to meet his client.[29] The *kāhin*, as described by the late eighth century and by later authors, was thus a localized holy man and the object of visits, as saints and their tombs became centers of pilgrimage (*ziyāra*) in popular Islam.[30] The *kāhin*, though, was not usually thought to reside in a temple; the temple personnel had other names (especially *sādin*), and they seem to have used divinatory accessories, like arrows, instead of being ecstatic seers.[31] The *kāhin* is described as living alone, often in a numinous place, like

---

[28] This does not necessarily show that the qurʾānic text originated within the framework of *kāhin* language, as the reverse is also possible. Knowing that Muḥammad was said by the Mekkans to be a *kāhin*, as the Qurʾān itself testifies (e.g., Qur. 52:29), the later commentators were prone to imagine that the *kāhin* dicta must have resembled these parts of the Qurʾān. Examples of preserved, but most probably inauthentic *kāhin* texts appear with French translations in Fahd, *Divination*, 162–69.

[29] The notable exception are stories in which the king, as in the story of Shiqq and Saṭīḥ, or the *shaykh* lets the *kāhin* be brought to him. Even in this case, the initiative of traveling does not come from the *kāhin* himself.

[30] One wonders whether the *kāhin* institution was smoothly Islamicized into a saint (*walī*) cult or whether there was a break in the tradition.

[31] See, in general, Fahd, *Divination*, 91–176. The references in Julius Wellhausen, *Reste arabischen Heidentums* (2d ed.; Berlin and Leipzig: Walter de Gruyter, 1927), 131, 134, and 143 (cf. Fahd, *Divination*, 94), to *kāhins* active in a sanctuary and speaking in the name of the divinity are vague and inconclusive, and are caused by Wellhausen's wish to identify *kāhin* with *kōhēn* and to show their Common Semitic priestly origin. Wellhausen's book suffers in general from his strong comparativist starting point. Wellhausen presupposes that Arabian religious life resembled the Common Semitic situation and can be used to reconstruct it. He accordingly sees traces of an earlier system, in which one might find little evidential value. Out of the scraps of information concerning the pre-Islamic period, one may build a plethora of hypothetical structures, some of which resemble the structures of other Semitic peoples, some not. Another problem in Wellhausen's book is that the complexity of the source material was fully realized more than half a century after Wellhausen wrote. Consequently, Wellhausen's use of sources is far too optimistic.

the one who, according to the *Sirah* (1:181/92), lived on a mountaintop, from whence he descended to meet his clients.

Survival of the *kāhin* institution is not in our sources, but the situation may have been similar to the institution of *riwāya,* in which the transmitter (*rāwī*) is said to have followed his master before becoming a poet (*shāʿir*) himself. Yet there should not be speculation about regular schools of *kāhin*s on the peninsula, since such an activity—besides not being mentioned in the sources—would more likely have been found around temples and their cults.

Likewise, we are told next to nothing of the *kāhin*s' possible ecstatic techniques. In the biography of Muḥammad, we come across both incubation and wrapping oneself in a cloth (see below), and it is possible that the *kāhin* used similar techniques; at least one of the *ridda* prophets, Ṭulayḥa, is described as prophesying while wrapped in a cloth.[32] The problem is that, when sources tell of such procedures, one remains uncertain whether the reports mirror the Qurʾān and the *Sirah* or preserve independent material. As shown by many studies, much of the explanatory material has been inferred from the qurʾānic text and does not represent any independent tradition.

In any case, the *kāhin* must have been a shamanlike visionary who forced his familiar spirit to descend upon him; otherwise he could not have served his clients. The Arabian sources tell of both male and female *kāhin*s. The former outnumber the latter in the *kāhin* narratives, but how closely this reflects the pre-Islamic situation is not clear. If the well-documented institution of Arabic queens in the earliest documents[33] relates to the *kāhin* institution, as suggested by Fahd,[34] then we might have a more predominantly female origin for the system.

---

32 *The Conquest of Arabia* (vol. 10 of *The History of al-Ṭabarī;* trans. Fred McGraw Donner; Bibliotheca Persica; Albany: State University of New York Press, 1988), 65–66. I give references only to the translation (abbreviated as Tabari), as the pagination of the original appears in the margins. The other volumes used are 6: *Muḥammad at Mecca,* trans. W. Montgomery Watt and M. V. McDonald (1993); 9: *The Last Years of the Prophet,* trans. Ismail K. Poonawala (1990); and 29: *Al-Manṣūr and al-Mahdī,* trans. Hugh Kennedy (1990).

33 See, e.g., Israel Ephʿal, *The Ancient Arabs: Nomads on the Borders of the Fertile Crescent, Ninth–Fifth Centuries B.C.* (Jerusalem: Magnes Press; Leiden: Brill, 1982), index, s.v. "Arab, *queen.*"

34 Fahd, *Divination,* 98–102.

The preponderance of male *kāhins* in the legends might even be an Islamic development, but these ideas are purely hypothetical.[35]

Were the *kāhins*, then, prophets? The answer depends on the definition of prophecy; if we presuppose that a prophet should have a distinctive message,[36] the *kāhin* fails to qualify. Yet as an intermediary between the divine—or at least the numinous—and the human, the *kāhin* does fill the gap. Despite their different social settings, one cannot draw a line between the functions of, for example, the Assyrian prophets[37] and the *kāhins*. The whole of Arabian prophecy grows out of *kihāna*. The *kāhin* has been seen as the spiritual and even as the political leader of his tribe, yet this role hardly manifests itself in the *kāhin* stories. The *kāhin* indicated prestige, and he may have been taken along to battlefields, but there is virtually no reliable evidence for him having been the leader of the tribe. It may be that the role of Muḥammad himself in Medina, as described by the *Sirah*, influenced this view, but, as we shall see, it may be hazardous to see in Muḥammad a "prophet and statesman."[38]

The Career of Muḥammad

This was the situation on the peninsula when Muḥammad started his career. In scholarly literature, based on the Islamic tradition, Muḥammad has been seen as the prophet of his native town, Mekka, who there came into contact with monotheists, Jews or Christians, from whom he received an impetus. Thus his invocation has been seen as a result of his becoming aware of a monotheist tradition.[39]

The earliest layers of the Qurʾān do not, however, support such a

---

[35] One might mention the Berber Kāhina, who in the late seventh century led her tribe against the Arabs; see M. Talbi, *"al-kāhina," Encyclopaedia of Islam*, vol. 4. For the female prophets in Assyria, see Nissinen, "The Socioreligious Role of the Neo-Assyrian Propets," in this volume.

[36] See Petersen, "Defining Prophecy and Prophetic Literature," in this volume.

[37] See in general Martti Nissinen, *References to Prophecy in Neo-Assyrian Sources* (SAAS 7; Helsinki: Neo-Assyrian Text Corpus Project, 1998), and Simo Parpola, *Assyrian Prophecies* (SAA 9; Helsinki: Helsinki University Press, 1997), as well as Nissinen's article in this volume.

[38] W. Montgomery Watt, *Muhammad: Prophet and Statesman* (Oxford: Oxford University Press, 1961).

[39] For a somewhat dated analysis, see Richard Bell, *The Origin of Islam in its Christian Environment* (Cunning Lectures, Edinburgh University, 1925; London: Frank Cass 1926).

view, as the biblical material is almost nonexistent in the earliest surahs. On the basis of the Qurʾān, it would seem more probable that Muḥammad started his career as an Arab prophet, who only later came into contact with Jews and, marginally, Christians. This reading is also supported by a reconsideration of the biographical material (see below). Thus, the immediate context from which Muḥammad emerged as a prophet has to be considered as Arabian prophecy.[40]

The career of Muḥammad brings to light a new dimension of the system of inspired holy men on the peninsula. There is much reason to suggest that Muḥammad originally was an itinerant prophet with a moral message, traveling on the peninsula—or at least in the Ḥijāz—before finally finding his community in Yathrib (later known as Medina). It was then that he started to be strongly influenced by the biblical tradition.[41] He was, furthermore, not alone in this tradition but had colleagues and competitors. Although we do not know the extent of the other prophetic movements, we know at least that Muḥammad was not unique. Among Islamic authors, Muḥammad was unique in his true prophecy.

Muḥammad is the best known of these prophets, even though the source-critical problems in his biography are not to be underestimated, and every reading of his life, whether conservative or revisionist, remains, for the time being, hypothetical. In brief, the traditional history tells us that the Prophet was born in Mekka into a prominent family around 570 and, having come into contact with monotheists, started his prophetic career around 610. He preached in Mekka for some ten to twelve years. As he met opposition from the leading Mekkans, he made contacts with bedouin tribes, which used to come to the central sanctuary of the peninsula, the Kaʿba, every year. He is also credited with having made an abortive attempt at *hijra* to the neighboring town of aṭ-Ṭāʾif in 619, but he was rejected and had to return to Mekka. He stayed in Mekka until his *hijra* to Yathrib in 622,

40 This is not to deny that some knowledge of Judaism and perhaps Christianity had already filtered through to the peninsula, not only in the time of Muḥammad but during earlier centuries. The Jewish presence especially had made itself felt for centuries, if not from the times of Nabū-nāʾid, then after the destruction of the Second Temple. Yet Gordon Darnell Newby, *A History of the Jews of Arabia: From Ancient Times to Their Eclipse under Islam* (Studies in Comparative Religion; Columbia: University of South Carolina Press, 1988), overdoes his case in trying to demonstrate the pervasiveness of the Jewish presence on the peninsula.

41 I am preparing a new analysis of Muḥammad's early life.

after which he became the leader of both his community (*umma*) and, eventually, of the whole town.

When working with the Qurʾān and the oldest version of his life, the *Sirah* by Ibn Hishām—dating from the early ninth century and closely based on the late-eighth-century *Sirah* by Ibn Isḥāq—the above picture of Muḥammad starts crumbling, and its chronological framework becomes improbable.[42] First, the earliest layers of the Qurʾān show no Jewish or Christian influence. It is too much even to speak of a monotheistic message in the earliest surahs; more than anything, they are monolatric. It is also startling that the only things we know about Muḥammad's life in the early period are legendary,[43] except for a few details which mostly point outside Mekka, many of them to Yathrib.[44] Combined with the fact that the majority of events situated in Mekka

---

42 It has long been known that the *Sirah* material was first transmitted in tiny narrative units, the *akhbār*, with little if any chronological frame. In theory, a radical rereading of the material should not be surprising. For the *akhbār* form of historical writing, see Franz Rosenthal, *A History of Muslim Historiography* (second revised edition; Leiden: Brill, 1968), 66–71.

43 Perusing relevant pages in either *Sirah* (1:136–2:99/66–227) or *Tabari* (especially vol. 6 of the translation) is enough to demonstrate this fact. The main events of Muḥammad's earliest years mentioned in *Tabari* are the impending sacrifice of his father, ʿAbdallāh, and the miraculous conception (6:1–8); the recognition of Muḥammad, in several versions, as the future prophet by the Syrian monk Baḥīrā and by another monk (6:44–48); Muḥammad's marriage to Khadīja, not located specifically in Mekka (one of the few events lacking religious motifs) (6:48–51); the rebuilding of the Kaʿba (6:51–59); and invocation (6:67–80). Afterward, the prophet's life becomes less based on religious themes, but there are few details, and these, moreover, tend to be used several times. Typically, one event is narrated twice, and the narrator states how many years passed between the two. An obvious example are the two pledges of ʿAqaba (6:122–138). There should be one year between these two events, but the situation in Mekka seems meanwhile to freeze. Likewise, very little seems to happen during the boycott (6:105–114), yet we are told that it "continued for two or three years" (6:106). Had the boycott, if it ever existed, taken so long, it is curious that there is nothing in the Qurʾān dealing with it.

44 The following examples are from *Tabari*. In the search for a *kāhina* to give a verdict on ʿAbdallāh, Muḥammad's father, ʿAbdallāh is taken from the Kaʿba while still a boy, first to Yathrib and from there to meet the *kāhina* (6:4). In one version of the legendary story of the conception, ʿAbdallāh is said to have been stained with clay or mud. As the translators note (6:6, n. 6), this passage has been interpreted as a reference to agriculture, which should not have been much practiced in Mekka—Yathrib, instead, was the area's main agricultural center (6:6). ʿAbdallāh dies in Yathrib and is buried there (6:8–9). Muḥammad's grandfather is said to have grown up in Yathrib (6:9–15). The opening of the breast happens, according to the most famous version, among the bedouin (see *Sirah* 1:144–149/69–73; in *Tabari* 6:75 this event is situated in the valley of Mekka). Setting the childhood

are either legendary or undatable, this necessitates rethinking the early location for Muḥammad. Muḥammad's genealogy also seems problematic. Besides legends (*Tabari* 6:1–9), nothing is known of his father, ʿAbdallāh, whose name, meaning "the servant of God," is often used in later texts when the real name is unknown. In the earliest literature, *ʿabdallāh* and the respective feminine *amatallāh* are used generically. Likewise, Muḥammad lacks brothers or sisters, and both of his parents are reported to have died when he was very young, his father, according to most traditions, before he was born. The existence of his grandfather ʿAbdalmuṭṭalib seems to have been doubted already by Frants Buhl.[45] In any case, the lack of (known) close relatives made Muḥammad's early life open to manipulation. This was easier than in Jesus' case, whose mother and a brother, James, played roles in the early community, yet whose genealogy and childhood were completely rewritten within a few decades of his death.[46]

It is not necessary to go into further detail. The main facts are as follows: the Mekkan provenance of Muḥammad and his affiliation with the main tribe of Mekka, the Quraysh, rests either on legends or the simple statements of the sources, with little evidence or detail. Except for events directly before the *hijra*, Muḥammad's life in Mekka is almost a blank. Its chronology seems arbitrary and may, in fact, be based on numerical speculation, as pointed out by Rubin.[47] The later association of the Prophet with the Quraysh would not be unique in a pre-Islamic tribal system in which lineage could be adjusted to comply with a new situation, and in which outsiders were admitted into a family for political reasons. The strong association of Muḥammad with Mekka

---

of Muḥammad in the strongly Jewish town of Yathrib would create more problems than it solves: Why was his early message, if he grew up in Yathrib, not already heavily Judaicized? More than anything, this example shows how confused the sources are as to his place of origin.

45 "ʿAbd al-Muṭṭalib," in *Handwörterbuch des Islam* (ed. A. J. Wensinck and J. H. Kramers; Leiden: Brill, 1941).

46 Muḥammad's obscure genealogy might be interpreted to place his origin outside the mainstream of Islamic history, perhaps outside the Ḥijāz. There are other possible explanations, including low origins—if Qur. 93:6 is a personal reminiscence, Muḥammad may have been an orphan—or perhaps the noncommitment of his family to the case of Islam. One need only remember the embarrassing cases of al-ʿAbbās and Abū Ṭālib, whose offspring started ascending toward leadership of the new Islamic state and had to explain their ancestors' stubborn refusal to convert early enough.

47 Rubin, *Eye of the Beholder*, 189–214.

finds its *Sitz im Leben* in the late-seventh-century emphasis on Mekka and its sanctuary, the Kaʿba, as the holy places of Islam. At this time the Arab background of the religion began to be emphasized as a counterweight to Jerusalem and the earlier monotheistic traditions.[48] The main deity of the Kaʿba, Hubal, is not mentioned in the Qurʾān[49] and is almost invisible in the surrounding explanatory material, as if his cult had had no influence on the life of Muḥammad and his enemies. Reading the *Sirah* and the Qurʾān, one would never conclude that Muḥammad had grown up in the cultic center of Hubal.[50] My main point, though—whether Muḥammad came from Quraysh or not—is that his early activity before the *hijra* has been misunderstood. The sources claim that he was active for some twelve years in Mekka before his *hijra*, but when studying the details this period seems to evaporate.

In the *Sirah* there are realistic details from the end of the Mekkan period. Almost all of these center on Muḥammad's activity during one

---

48 As an aside, I draw attention to the fact that Mekka did not have a special role in the subsequent history of the Islamic community. The conquest of Mekka appears in the *Sirah* as the goal of the Prophet and as the final victory of his military activities, but the *Sirah* itself grossly contradicts such an assumption. The military success in Mekka was remarkable, but it was not the final aim of the new state, which continued its campaigns after the conquest as if nothing had happened. Mekka was just one victory among many others; only later was it made the central event in the holy history of Islam.

49 The three female deities, al-ʿUzzā, Allat, and Manāt, are mentioned both in the Qurʾān (53:19) and in the biographical material, as in the famous *ḥadīth,* according to which Muhammad had made offerings to al-ʿUzzā before his invocation. See Hishām al-Kalbī, *Kitāb al-aṣnām* (ed. Muḥammad ʿAbdalqādir Aḥmad and Aḥmad Muḥammad ʿUbayd; Cairo: Maktabat an-nahḍa al-Miṣrīya, n.d.), 34; a similar story has been studied by M. J. Kister, "'A Bag of Meat': A Study of an Early Ḥadith," *BSOAS* 33 (1970): 267–75, reprinted in M. J. Kister, *Studies in Jāhiliyya and Early Islam* (London: Variorum Reprints, 1980). Al-ʿUzzā is strongly linked with aṭ-Ṭāʾif (e.g., al-Kalbī, *Kitāb al-aṣnām,* 31), another town which plays a role in the *Sirah.*

50 The equation by Wellhausen, *Reste,* 75, of Hubal with *rabb hādhā l-bayt* or Allah is unwarranted. There are stray mentions that deny the Mekkan origin of Muḥammad, but these are inconclusive; not too much weight should be given to them. Thus, in some versions of a tradition, quoted in Suliman Bashear, *Arabs and Others in Early Islam* (Studies in Late Antiquity and Early Islam 8; Princeton, N.J.: Darwin Press, 1997), 50 and n. 35, ʿUmar wonders about the eloquence of Muḥammad, stating that "you are not from among us," or, in another version, "you did not come up from among us" (*lam takhruj min bayni aẓhurinā*). Such remarks may be seen, depending on the scholar, as remnants of original information which have escaped the general harmonization in the historical material, or as careless mistakes which have no evidential value.

mawsim. Whether this "festive season" is to be equated with the pre-Islamic pilgrimage (*ḥajj*) need not detain us, but it is striking that in Mekka the activity of Muḥammad, not unlike that of Jesus in Jerusalem, seems to be limited to one festive season—the traditional biography assumes that his activity covered several years, and the *mawsims* to which the text refers should thus belong to different years. Also realistic is that Muḥammad is said to have made contact with bedouin tribes. These contacts are schematically related in the *Sirah* and are said to have happened during the *ḥajj* (see, e.g., *Tabari* 6:120–122).

It is now well-known that the importance of the pre-Islamic *ḥajj* has been much exaggerated. If we still want to believe in historical grounding for contacts with bedouin tribes, it would be possible to take them as reminiscences of Muḥammad's itinerant career among the tribes. When later tradition set Muḥammad in Mekka by later tradition, these encounters had to take place in the Holy City, as it was now regarded. As Muḥammad no longer came to the tribes, the tribes had to come to Muḥammad. Muḥammad is also reported to have journeyed to aṭ-Ṭāʾif, the cultic center of al-ʿUzzā (*Sirah* 2:29–31/192–193). In the *Sirah,* this *hijra* is set after the lengthy early period in Mekka, which had led Muḥammad into conflict with the local aristocracy. Thus, he would have left his native town for aṭ-Ṭāʾif,[51] but as the early period of Muḥammad in Mekka is known only from legends, we might speculate that he was in aṭ-Ṭāʾif before the activity in Mekka.[52] That Muḥammad was followed to aṭ-Ṭāʾif only by Abū Bakr, the future first caliph, underlines the lack of a community[53] and would justify dating the event near the beginning of his career.

Thus, we might build his early life from the following elements, in this order: vague childhood reminiscences, all pointing outside of

---

51 The *Sirah* dates this toward the end of the Mekkan period, but Muḥammad is shown as virtually unknown in a town which should have had close relations with Mekka, where the *Sirah* claims that Muḥammad had lived for some fifty years and acted as a prophet for ten years. Yet he was unknown in aṭ-Ṭāʾif.

52 It is impossible to build a coherent travelogue based on the meager information in the *Sirah,* but I cannot resist pointing to the fact that, while aṭ-Ṭāʾif is located southeast of Mekka, Yathrib is north of Mekka. Thus, there would have been an ideal route from aṭ-Ṭāʾif to Yathrib, via Mekka. It goes without saying that I draw attention to this route only half-seriously.

53 Note that Abū Bakr's role can easily be explained by the wish to give as much merit as possible to the first successor of Muḥammad.

Mekka; contacts with bedouin tribes; appearance in aṭ-Ṭāʾif; a period in Mekka during a *mawsim.* In Mekka he found an insufficient following and finally left for Yathrib—perhaps against the will of the Mekkans, who are depicted as unwilling to let Muḥammad leave for Yathrib.[54] In choosing this reading of his life, many details would fall nicely into place: the limited number of nonlegendary events in his early life; the biblicalization of his message after an initial "Arab" period; the references to places outside Mekka (see n. 44 above); the lack of close relatives in Mekka; and so on.

To this, one might add that the non-Muslim literary evidence strongly favors Yathrib as the native town of Muḥammad and does not mention Mekka in this context. The mid-eighth-century Syriac chronicler, quoted by Dionysius of Tellmaḥre, wrote:

> This Muḥammad, while in the age and stature of youth, began to go up and down from his town of Yathrib to Palestine for the business of buying and selling. While so engaged in the country, he saw the belief in one God and it was pleasing to his eyes.[55]

While there is an obvious tendency to show the Christian origin of Muḥammad's "heresy," this text does show that the author, who, it might

---

54 The great secrecy in which the *hijra* is said to have been planned and executed (*Sirah* 2:39–93/197–231; *Tabari* 6:139–150) is difficult to explain if we accept the traditional version of Muḥammad's life. If Muḥammad had been annoying the Mekkans, his departure would have been more than welcome (it is a wisdom of hindsight when the sources say that the Mekkans were afraid of his later military actions—that would have been unprecedented in tribal history). Muḥammad seems, on the contrary, to have become a showpiece of the tribe, and his departure meant a lowering of prestige: Mekka lost its Prophet. That Muḥammad left Mekka, in light of the early parts of the Qurʾān, would have been because he did not find enough enthusiasm among the Mekkans. The Qurʾān does not mention serious persecutions but merely a stubborn refusal to obey the divine message.

55 Translation quoted from Robert G. Hoyland, *Seeing Islam as Others Saw It: A Survey and Evaluation of Christian, Jewish, and Zoroastrian Writings on Early Islam* (Studies in Late Antiquity and Early Islam 13; Princeton, N.J.: Darwin Press, 1997), 130. For the relations among the various texts, see ibid., 400–409. The passage concerning Muḥammad and his trips to Palestine seems ultimately to derive from Jacob of Edessa (d. 708) and his *Chronicle;* cf. ibid., 405, n. 62. This passage was commented on by Sebastian Brock, "Syriac Views of Emergent Islam," in *Studies on the First Century of Islamic Society* (ed. G. H. A. Juynboll; Carbondale: Southern Illinois University Press, 1982), 9–21, 199–203 (reprinted as *Syriac Perspectives on Late Antiquity* [London: Variorum Reprints, 1984], 11–12), although he did not comment on the mention of Yathrib in this context.

be added, writes before the earliest Islamic accounts, does not know of links between Muḥammad and Mekka.

In the Syriac chronicle *Ad annum 724*, probably deriving from an early Arabic original,[56] the list of the Arab rulers is prefaced as follows:[57] "A notice on the life of *Mḥmṭ* the messenger of God, after he had entered his city [viz., Yathrib] and three months before he entered it, from his first year." The passage implies that he had a career for three months before he came to Yathrib, which would fit my hypothesis of a short period of activity in Mekka nicely. The text speaks unequivocally of Muḥammad's life (i.e., career) before his *hijra*, not of the *hijrī* dating. This could also be seen as an allusion to the *hijrī* calendar, which starts two months and a few days before Muḥammad's arrival in Yathrib.[58] Thus the passage remains inconclusive.

Removing the legends and critically analyzing the life of Muḥammad before the *hijra* leads toward a picture of Muḥammad as an itinerant prophet, preaching and conveying a moral message to various tribes and towns. Where he came from originally remains obscure. Yathrib after the *hijra* is the proper scene for the biblicalization of Muḥammad's message, as the city was undoubtedly one of the peninsula's Jewish strongholds.[59] Muḥammad became conscious there of earlier monotheist traditions, and his prophecy started changing according to these models. In a word, he had been an Arabian prophet, but in Yathrib he became a link in the monotheist *Heilsgeschichte* and became closely associated with the biblical prophets, as Muslims understood them.

---

56 Hoyland, *Seeing Islam*, 396. Such chronological lists are now usually taken to represent the earliest layer of Arabic historical writing, and thus are presumed more accurate that the later *akhbār* (e.g., Patricia Crone, *Slaves on Horses: The Evolution of the Islamic Polity* [Cambridge: Cambridge University Press, 1980]).

57 Hoyland, *Seeing Islam*, 395.

58 See ibid., 396, who explains this in this way, but it remains disturbing that the gap between these two dates is actually less than two and a half months. See also *Tabari* 6:162.

59 Note that while keeping the overall relative framework of Nöldeke's chronology, I do not accept his absolute chronology. The periods Mekka II and Mekka III may have to be situated in Yathrib and, if I am correct in assuming that Muḥammad was an itinerant prophet, the surahs of the first "Mekkan" period might partly have originated elsewhere.

Muḥammad's Prophetic Experience

Muḥammad had two kinds of prophetic experiences during his career. The main type, the *audition,* consisted of prophetic messages codified in the Qurʾān[60] and which later, in Yathrib, came under heavy biblical influence. In later literature, several stories describe how Muḥammad received these messages, but the stories are far from reliable and do not offer a solid basis for further analysis. Wrapping oneself in a cloth is an ecstatic technique which seems to find corroboration in the Qurʾān.[61] A familiar spirit (*tābiʿ*), the supernatural being who descends on the visionary, would have been the pre-Islamic model for Muḥammad's visions, and this is how his visions would at first have been understood. Only later, with the biblicalization of his prophecy, does the intermediatory angel, Gabriel or Isrāfīl, take the place of the one who brings the divine message.

The other type of prophetic activity consisted of *dreams and visions.*[62] These are sometimes alluded to in the Qurʾān (e.g., 8:43: dream) but the Qurʾān tells regrettably little about them. The most interesting description in the Qurʾān comes in Surah 53, which tells of two visions. In one, the text speaks of a numen[63] which Muḥammad saw descending nearby, and in the other vision, experienced near "the Utmost Lote-Tree,"[64] he saw something which "covered" the tree. Dreams have a clear role in some parts of the *Sirah.* Especially interesting is that, in

---

60 The position of Wansbrough, *Quranic Studies,* is extreme. Wansbrough sees the Qurʾān as a compilation of some two centuries and as the product of several local traditions. Wansbrough's position has found few wholehearted supporters and is, in fact, untenable. It is built on a strong desire to see the Qurʾān as parallel to biblical texts, partly to justify Wansbrough in using methods of biblical scholarship to study it.

61 *Muzzammil* (Qur. 73:1) and *muddaththir* (Qur. 74:1), both roughly meaning "one who has wrapped himself in a cloth." The concomitant stories in the commentaries are of dubious authenticity.

62 See W. Montgomery Watt, *Muhammad's Mecca: History in the Quran* (Islamic Surveys; Edinburgh: Edinburgh University Press, 1988), 54–68. Watt has done valuable work on early Islam, but his attitude toward the material is very conservative.

63 The standard interpretations speak of Gabriel or God, depending on the commentator; the text does not specify what Muḥammad actually saw.

64 This scene later was added to the story of Muḥammad's ascension to heaven, but in the original context this interpretation is not possible. The story of the celestial ascent of Muḥammad has to be dated no earlier than the late seventh century; its *Sitz im Leben* is the multireligious milieu following the conquests (see Hämeen-Anttila, "Descent").

most of these dream stories, Muḥammad is described as a passive medium or intermediary; it is Abū Bakr who explains the dreams and takes an active role. One example may be sufficient.[65] In *Sirah* 4:110–111/590, during the siege of aṭ-Ṭāʾif, Muḥammad tells his dream to Abū Bakr. He dreamed that he had been given a bowl full of butter, but a rooster pecked at it and spilled it. Abū Bakr interprets the dream, saying that Muḥammad will not reach his aim that day. Muḥammad agrees, retrieving his troops.

Muḥammad does not emerge from these stories as a statesman and leader—a role that caliphal propaganda since the end of the seventh century wanted to give him—but as a holy man who follows the tribe in its warlike activities and provides supernatural guidance for the leaders through an oracle or ominous dream, the interpretation of which is left for others. The story is told in the *Sirah* as if Abū Bakr only voiced doubts Muḥammad himself already had, and it is eventually Muḥammad who decides how to act. But this is how one would suppose the story to have been modified, once Muḥammad's central role in Islam had developed into a dogma. Yet it does remain conspicuous how often Abū Bakr is depicted in this interpretative role, as if it were up to him to interpret Muḥammad's dreams and to draw practical conclusions.

There is also a story that implies incubation. In some versions of the *isrāʾ*, the night journey[66] starts from the Kaʿba, where the Prophet is sleeping. As the story of the *isrāʾ* and the concomitant *miʿrāj,* ascension to heaven, is of later origin,[67] it is not possible to give much weight to it.

The *Sirah* contains prophetic dreams from others, too. Perhaps the most intriguing is the portentous dream of the Prophet's aunt,[68] ʿĀtika bint ʿAbdalmuṭṭalib, who had remained pagan (*Sirah* 2:212–214/290).[69] Her dream was welcomed with scorn by pagan Mekkans,

---

65 Another dream from the final period of Muḥammad's activities appears in *Sirah* 4:63/776–777 (no. 815). Note also the dream in *Sirah* 2:230/300.

66 See Qur. 17:1 and the legendary material attached.

67 See, e.g., Hämeen-Anttila, "Descent."

68 That is, if we accept the traditional genealogy of Muḥammad.

69 The dream of ʿĀtika has been also discussed by Fahd, *Divination,* 279–81. Dreams also retained their importance in later Islamic culture. An interesting case of a dream as a medium of official propaganda is al-Maʾmūn's Aristotelian dream, discussed in Dimitri Gutas, *Greek Thought, Arabic Culture: The Graeco-Arabic Translation Movement in Baghdad and Early ʿAbbāsid Society (2nd–4th/8th–10th centuries)* (Lon-

and her brother, al-ʿAbbās ibn ʿAbdalmuṭṭalib was rebuked: "Are you not satisfied that your men should play the prophet that your women should do so also?" As the story is no more reliable than other information concerning Muḥammad's life, one has to be hesitant about accepting it—yet it is worth noticing.

The Context for Muḥammad's Prophecy

What seems to have distinguished Muḥammad from other Arab prophets is that in Yathrib he was influenced by the biblical tradition, which made him see himself as different from and more than other Arab prophets. This evolution finally led to the birth of a new monotheistic religion. With this change of focus, Muḥammad set himself in a new paradigm. Instead of an itinerant Arab prophet, he became the God of Israel's messenger to humankind—or, more probably, to the Arabs only.[70] The composition of a Holy Book also resulted from this redirection as the text of the Qurʾān testifies. When his biography was written more than a century later, this final biblical phase of prophecy was retrojected to the beginning of his career.

Muḥammad was not the only Arab prophet, *kāhins* apart. We have information about many of his competitors, and after his death there was no abrupt discontinuation of Arabian prophecy. To be sure, the most intimate followers of Muḥammad did not claim to have succeeded him in his prophetic function, and even the Marwānid Umayyads, especially ʿAbdalmalik (r. 685–705), who conceived the caliph as a divinely authorized king in Sasanian style, never claimed to be prophets. For them, though, the caliph, the vice-regent of God on earth, was in fact a higher functionary than even the prophet Muḥammad.[71]

We have scattered information on Muḥammad's main competitor,

---

don and New York: Routledge, 1998), 95–104. Dreams and their interpretation have been discussed by Fahd, *Divination*, 247–367, who has also collected an impressive list of oneirocritic manuscripts. See also Friedmann, "Finality," 199–202, and Leah Kinberg, "Literal Dreams and Prophetic Ḥadīṯs in Classical Islam: A Comparison of Two Ways of Legitimation," *Der Islam* 70 (1993): 279–300.

70 Later Islamic tradition shows unequivocally how Christianity and Judaism were seen as acceptable religions: Islam was no missionary religion. Similarly, a late passage in the Qurʾān (2:62)sees these religions as potentially leading to salvation—despite later attempts to interpret the passage differently.

71 See Crone and Hinds, *God's Caliph*, 24–42.

Musaylima (*al-Kadhdhāb,* "the Liar"), from Banū Ḥanīfa, who is said to have met Muḥammad, as well as on the prophetess Sajāḥi and a few others, the so-called *ridda*[72] prophets. What these prophets preached, and to what extent they had been influenced by biblical tradition or by Muḥammad, remains hard to evaluate. The classical sources are more or less unanimous that they had a universal message—concocted from Christianity and travesties of Muḥammad's message, if we are to believe the Islamic sources. They did have a message, most probably similar to that of Muḥammad—except that their message is purposefully distorted by the sources. Some of the prophets may, in fact, have seen themselves as Muḥammad's successors, and probably conceived of themselves as Muslims. Thus, when Muḥammad died, his place was open for Musaylima and other prophets. The idea may sound unfamiliar to Muslims as well as to Western scholars who have adopted classical thinking, but it is quite natural. Why should prophecy have ended with the death of one prophet?[73]

The *ridda* prophets are usually said to have led the *ridda* movements, but this is probably not accurate. It seems that they personified the *ridda* movements more than they led them. The stories do not consistently show them as the leaders of their tribes, and many sources draw attention to the fact that there were more noble—and hence poten-

---

[72] The term *ridda* means "apostasy"; from the Islamic point of view, these prophets and their tribes, which had succumbed to the Islamic state of Yathrib, committed apostasy when they refused to accept the supremacy of Yathrib after Muḥammad's death. It should be noted, though, that the concept of *ridda* is mistaken. The military activities of the Islamic state did not stop, and different tribal confederations always used the opportunity to counterattack Yathrib. The *ridda* wars were the direct continuation of wars in the final years of Muḥammad, and a direct predecessor of the conquests (*futūḥ*). The tripartite scheme (conquest of Mekka—*ridda—futūḥ*) derives from later historians, not the material itself. The term *ridda* is also misunderstood from another point of view. We have no proof that the *ridda* prophets conceived of themselves in opposition to Muḥammad's new religion. They opposed the leadership of Yathrib after the death of Muḥammad. *Ridda* prophets are discussed in all histories of the Islamic state after the death of Muḥammad. Ibn Aʿtham al-Kūfī's *Kitāb al-Futūḥ* (1388–1395; ed. Muḥammad ʿAbdalmʿīd Khān; vols. 1–8; As-Silsila al-jadīda min maṭbūʿāt Dāʾirat al-maʿārif al-ʿuthmānīya 9/12/1–8; Ḥaydarābād: Maṭbaʿat Dāʾirat al-maʿārif al-ʿuthmānīya, 1968–1975; repr., Beirut: *Dār an-nadwa al-jadīda,* n.d.) contains a large selection of these stories with examples of—obviously invented—prophetic dicta of the *ridda* prophets (1:1–87).

[73] Stroumsa's discussion of Manichaean prophecy, in "'Seal of the Prophets,'" is relevant as a parallel case.

tially more influential—men among their followers.[74] Musaylima is the best-known of these prophets.[75] According to Muslim sources, he was the prophet of the Banū Ḥanīfa in Yamāma, and claimed to be receiving revelations. The text of some of these revelations has been transmitted,[76] but their authenticity is dubious. Some of them are fanciful inventions, concocted to show the emptiness of Musaylima's false "revelations" and to contrast them with the noble message of Muḥammad. The following (*Tabari* 10:109) is often quoted as authentic:[77]

> Oh frog, daughter of a frog, croak what you croak, your upper part is in the water and your lower part in the mud, do not bar any person drinking, nor make the water turbid.[78]

---

74 Thus, e.g., Abū ʿUbayd al-Qāsim ibn Sallām, *Kitāb an-nasab* (1410; ed. Maryam Muḥammad Khayraddarʿ; Dār al-Fikr, 1989), 352: "Muḥakkam al-Yamāma Ibn aṭ-Ṭufayl was more noble than Musaylima." In Ibn Aʿtham, *Futūḥ* 1:33, Muḥakkam is called Musaylima's vizier and "his man" (*ṣāḥib*); his role may have been similar to that of Abū Bakr in relation to Muḥammad. Like Muḥammad (*Sirah* 2:230/300), Ṭulayḥa is shown as supporting his troops behind the lines (Ibn Aʿtham, *Futuḥ* 1:14–15), not leading the battle but inspiring it with his presence.

75 The standard study of Musaylima is Dale F. Eickelmann, "Musaylima: An Approach to the Social Anthropology of Seventh-Century Arabia," *Journal of the Economic and Social History of the Orient* 10 (1967): 17–52, which is based mainly on secondary sources and is unsatisfactory. An in-depth study, which is still lacking, would take the Arab sources and their problems into full account; any lucid understanding of the *ridda* prophets' career presupposes the collection of all Islamic material pertinent to their lives, with sound source criticism.

76 E.g., in *Tabari* 10:108–109.

77 Another version appears in *Tabari* 10:133. As the text of these "revelations" was never canonized, it developed as wildly as any anecdotal material, without reaching fixed form. In Ibn Aʿtham's *Futūḥ* (1:29), a Ḥanafī contemporary of Musaylima is made to voice the opinion of Islamic authors: "You have heard the Qurʾān brought by Muḥammad. . . . How far his speech is from that of Musaylima the Liar!"

78 As an aside, one might draw attention to the anonymous Latin *Vita of 850*, translated by Kenneth B. Wolf in *Medieval Iberia: Readings from Christian, Muslim, and Jewish Sources* (ed. Olivia Remie Constable; Middle Ages Series; Philadelphia: University of Pennsylvania Press, 1997), 49. This source is, in general, well informed concerning Islam, and it describes Muḥammad's activity in the following words (words in brackets added): "The same false prophet [i.e., Muḥammad] composed psalms from the mouths of irrational animals, commemorating a red calf [the Surah of the Cow, 2]. He wove a story of spiderwebs for catching flies [reference to the Surah of the Spider, 29]. He composed certain sayings about the hoopoe [reference to the Surah of the Ant, 27:20] and the frog [*sic*]. . . . [H]e arranged other songs in his own style in honor of Joseph, Zachary and even the mother of the Lord, Mary [the Surah of Mary, 19]." All "psalms" and "songs" of Muḥammad are correct references to the Qurʾān, except for the reference to the

More credible are the passages which sound more religious (see, e.g., *Tabari* 10:93–95). These tend to closely resemble the earliest layers of the Qurʾān; whether they do so because they have been fabricated on the basis of the Qurʾān, or because they belong to the same tradition, is far from clear.

The few texts transmitted from the other prophets follow the Musaylima passages and have the same problems. Worth noticing, though, is the existence of a prophetess, Sajāḥi, although she is best known for the sexual insults heaped on her by later Muslims.[79] On the other hand, she is said (*Tabari* 10:93) to have known Christianity; the Taghlib tribe, with which she is associated, was at least partly Christianized.

Some of the *ridda* prophets were contemporary with Muḥammad. Islamic sources and tendentious history writing has not been able to hide that, for example, Musaylima was already active during the life of the prophet Muḥammad. These sources describe all the pseudoprophets as mere emulators of Muḥammad. Other prophets may have appeared only after Muḥammad had died, and they seem to have come, at least partly, from among the Muslims. The best known of these is Ṭulayḥa, who reconverted to Islam later in his life.[80] Ṭulayḥa and Musaylima, too, are said to have received messages through Gabriel,[81] but this may also be an extrapolation of Muḥammad's situation. On the other hand, in *Tabari* 9:167, Ṭulayḥa's divine intermediator is called Dhūʾn-Nūn; and in *Tabari* 10:112, the one who comes to Musaylima is ar-Raḥmān. The prolific and ever varying names do not engender much confidence.

---

frog, an animal which is nowhere mentioned. The same source mentions that "the spirit of error appeared to him in the form of a vulture," which Muḥammad said was the angel Gabriel (p. 48). Even this might be based on more than slander. In Ibn al-Munādī, *Malāḥim* 50 (Saṭīḥ Apocalypse), a raven (*ghurāb*) is reported to have brought messages to Saṭīḥ. Perhaps the *Vita* is transmitting Islamic materials originally purported to be used against pseudoprophets and turning them against Muḥammad himself. The question needs a separate study.

79 See, e.g., the famous poem no. 41 by al-Aghlab al-ʿIjlī (Jaakko Hämeen-Anttila, ed., *Five Rağaz Collections: Materials for the Study of Rağaz Poetry II* [StudOr 76; Helsinki: Societas Orientalis Fennica, 1995]). Contrary to the date usually given for the poet (d. 641), the poem, as well as the majority of other poems attributed to al-Aghlab, dates considerably later; al-Aghlab—or at least the author of this poem—is no contemporary of Sajāḥi.

80 See, e.g., *Tabari* 10:74. Sajāḥi, too, reconverted (*Tabari* 10:97), which shows how lightly the early Muslims took the matter.

81 Ibn Aʿtham, *Futūḥ* 1:10, 12, and 24; cf. *Tabari* 10:66.

In general, Islamic authors describe the *ridda* prophets as imitators of Muḥammad, but this is often mere fiction. It is, for example, improbable that Sajāḥi would have let the prayer call contain the formula "I testify that Sajāḥi is the prophetess of God" (*ashhadu anna Sajāḥi nabīyatu llāh*); the central role of Muḥammad in Islam and his place in the call to prayer hardly dates to this time. Likewise, al-Aswad[82] is called "an apostle of God" by his followers (*Tabari* 10:28), although in this case we might have a historical report, as there is no reason why other prophets would not have imitated the most successful prophet of Yathrib.

Some *ridda* prophets may have seen themselves as continuing the prophecy of Muḥammad. Thus, when Musaylima freed the followers of Sajāḥi from two of the five daily prayers Muḥammad had imposed on them (*Tabari* 10:95), the implication is that he continues the work of Muḥammad, instead of opposing or disclaiming it.[83] That his Islam was not what became accepted as orthodox Islam need not blind us to the fact that heresy and orthodoxy became defined only in time. Had Musaylima or some of the other *ridda* prophets succeeded, theirs would have been the orthodoxy.[84]

Paradigms of Arabian Prophecy

These abortive attempts to develop—or to continue—a full-grown model of continuous prophecy eventually failed. Whether these prophets had a model in earlier times is not clear. In any case, we have no reports of prophetic schools on the peninsula or of prophetic succession within a holy family. The only evidence which could be so interpreted is the above-mentioned passage concerning ʿĀtika, and it is too equivocal to be used as a basis for further hypotheses.[85]

---

[82] See, e.g., *Tabari* 9:165. Most of the information on these *ridda* prophets appears in the tenth volume of *Tabari*.

[83] One should not, though, forget that, in the earliest phase, the Muslims seem to have had three daily prayers (see Qur. 11:114; 50:39–40; 76:25–26). If there is a historical core to the three daily prayers for Sajāḥi's followers, this might have been an earlier practice. In that case, the "reduction" of the five prayers to three would be an etiology for the existing habit.

[84] Ar-Rajjāl (or ar-Raḥḥāl) was said to have been a knowledgeable Muslim, and he did not have scruples about following Musaylima after the death of Muḥammad (*Tabari* 10:107, 117).

[85] We also find stray remarks like that in Ibn Aʿtham, *Futūḥ* 1:4, in which Quraysh is referred to as *Ahl an-nubūwa,* "the people of prophecy." The passage

Prophecy on the Arabian Peninsula was not exclusively pagan and Arab in character. The *Sirah* is full of stories about Jewish and Christian holy men, as well as *ḥanīfs*[86] wandering on the peninsula, preaching or searching for the truth. These stories are told in Islamic literature as annunciation stories; the gist is predicting the Prophet soon to come. In addition to pagan prophets, there may have been a prophet, or at least a visionary, from among the Jews. The little-known and imperfectly understood Medinese Jew, Ṣāfī ibn Ṣayyād,[87] may have claimed to be a prophet. Ibn Ṣayyād was already active when Muḥammad met him, according to some stories. In ad-Dānī's *as-Sunan al-wārida* 1191–1200 (nos. 659–665),[88] there are seven *ḥadīths* concerning ibn Ṣayyād. Some of these *ḥadīths* show him as a *kāhin*. In no. 665,[89] the prophet Muḥammad tests him in traditional *kāhin* style ("I am keeping something hidden from you"). In others (nos. 661–662), Ibn Ṣayyād claims to be a messenger of God, equal to Muḥammad. In no. 662, he is depicted as a visionary who sees the throne of God on water, a vision familiar from Merkavah mysticism.[90]

Later authors saw the Antichrist in Ibn Ṣayyād: the *ḥadīths* about

may be interpreted innocuously (as the people among whom the last and final prophet appeared), but it does give room for a less orthodox reading (the people from among whom prophets in general arose). The *ḥadīth* according to which Muḥammad's son, Ibrāhīm, would have become a prophet had he not died in infancy (discussed in Friedmann, "Finality," 186–93) is of a later period, and even the existence of Ibrāhīm has lately been questioned; see Kaj Öhrnberg, "Māriya al-Qibṭiyya Unveiled," *StudOr* 55 (1984): 297–303.

86 A rather obscure term closely associated in the Qur'ān with Abraham; see, e.g., 3:67. The discussion of Watt, *Muhammad's Mecca*, 37–38, is relevant to the meaning of *ḥanīf*. I agree with Watt in doubting the existence of any "*ḥanīf* movement" before Islam.

87 The name is spelled in slightly different forms: Ibn Ṣā'id; Ibn aṣ-Ṣā'id; Ibn aṣ-Ṣayyād; etc. For more about Ibn Ṣayyād, see especially David Halperin, "The Ibn Ṣayyād Traditions and the Legend of al-Dajjāl," *JAOS* 96 (1976): 213–25, and Steven M. Wasserstrom, *Between Muslim and Jew: The Problem of Symbiosis under Early Islam* (Princeton: Princeton University Press, 1995), 77–82. In Ibn al-Munādī, *Malāḥim*, 222, there is an interesting story which has been overlooked by Halperin. According to the story, Ibn Ṣā'id was an Isfahanian Jew who went into occultation in order to return as the Antichrist.

88 In addition to ʿUthmān ibn Saʿīd ad-Dānī, *as-Sunan al-wārida fī l-fitan wa-ghawā'ilihā wa's-sāʿa wa-ashrāṭihā* (1416; ed. Riḍā'allāh Muḥammad Idrīs al-Mubārakfūrī; Riyadh: Dār al-ʿāṣima, 1995), and the sources used by Halperin, "Ibn Ṣayyād," see also Ibn al-Munādī, *Malāḥim*, index, s.vv. "Ibn Ṣā'id" and "Ibn Ṣayyād."

89 See Halperin, "Ibn Ṣayyād," 219.

90 See ibid., 217–18.

him are more interested in his apocalyptic role than in his earthly activities; consequently, the historical Ibn Ṣayyād tends to evade us.[91] It is almost impossible to say whether a person called Ibn Ṣayyād existed at the time of Muḥammad, but these relatively early testimonies imply that eighth-century scholars believed that a Jewish visionary or a prophet had been active in Medina in the seventh century. In any case, Ibn Ṣayyād was not an Arab prophet but an Arabic-speaking Jewish visionary (or messiah or prophet).

Thus there is considerable evidence for claiming that the prophets and soothsayers of the peninsula had two main paradigms. First, there was the local *kāhin*—at least some of whom are depicted as living in inaccessible places—visited both by his own tribe and by others when they were in need of an oracle. The second group consists of itinerant prophets and preachers, the holy men who traveled in search of an audience. These prophets had a message to convey and were respected, if not obeyed, due to their inherent authority as representatives of God and as channels for divine messages. Prophets are never tested in the stories in the same sense as the *kāhins*. They may produce signs (*āyāt*)—for Muslim authors, Muḥammad produced truthful signs, the "pseudoprophets" only legerdemain—but their authority ultimately derives from the divine message they convey. If the audience does not believe in the message and the signs adduced by the prophet, it is to their detriment. But if the client does not believe in the abilities of the *kāhin*, he is free to turn to another. The basic difference between the two types of prophets lies in the universality and content of their message. We are rarely told that *kāhins* did more than answer questions. They received their authority from their clients, not from the divinity they represented or from who expressed himself in the oracle. They were selected, tested, and, when they passed the test, their word was accepted. It was accepted because their clients needed a soothsayer or a neutral *ḥakam*, a supernaturally inspired judge, not because the *kāhin* had inherent authority as a representative of God.[92] The *kāhin* could be ignored, but not the prophet. Both types continued well into

---

91 Whether Ibn Ṣayyād was the Antichrist is heatedly debated in the *ḥadīths* I have quoted as well as in their various commentaries. The origin of this debate may have been confusion caused by the word *dajjāl*, which is used both for pseudoprophets and the Antichrist.

92 A group close to *kāhins* were the diviners. We have little reliable information on divinatory practices in pre-Islamic times. The *Sirah* (1:136–139/66–68) de-

Islamic times. The *kāhins* were attested in the peninsula up to the twentieth century, as reported especially from South Arabia. The other type, the itinerant prophet with a universal message, is less known, especially since Sunni Islam later denied the possibility of continuous prophecy after Muḥammad.[93]

After the conquest, the history of the peninsula remains almost undocumented, except for episodes that occurred mainly in the last two decades of the seventh century. Modern evidence shows that the *kāhins* continued their activities, especially among the bedouins, who never fully absorbed Islam and to a great extent retained their Arab thought-patterns and traces of Semitic paganism.[94] When the focus of Islam changed to the old cultural area of the Near East, mainly Palestine, Syria, and Iraq, prophecy became deeply influenced by local traditions. As is well-known, the centuries before Islam were a period of great religious activity, and several persons, both within Judaism and Christianity and on the margins, claimed to be receiving messages from God. The Elchasaites and the Manichaeans likely represent the most famous of these movements, but they were not the only ones. When the "Believers," as the early Muslims called themselves, conquered the region, a steady influx of converts started joining their ranks, bringing their cultural and religious heritages. The religion of Islam was taking fixed form slowly. Local versions tended to develop in different directions, and different prophetic traditions found their way into some forms of Islam. Our best sources for these are the later heresiographies and, to a lesser extent, later Shiite literature, which preserves traces of seventh- and eighth-century movements. Their ideas

---

scribes divination with arrows in the Kaʿba. For divination in general, see Fahd, *Divination.*

93 Prophets did continue appearing but were usually executed, unless their career as prophets could be marginalized. The *cause célèbre* of later prophets was the poet al-Mutanabbī (d. 965), who got his nickname "the would-be prophet," it is said, from a youthful adventure among bedouins. See, e.g., Wolfhart Heinrichs, "The Meaning of Mutanabbī," in *Poetry and Prophecy: The Beginnings of a Literary Tradition* (ed. James L. Kugel; Ithaca, N.Y.: Cornell University Press, 1990), 120–39 and 231–39.

94 On bedouin religiosity, see, e.g., Joseph Henninger, *Arabica Sacra: Aufsätze zur Religionsgeschichte Arabiens und seiner Randgebiete* (OBO 40; Göttingen: Vandenhoeck & Ruprecht, 1981). Note that the Antichrist is often said to find his followers among bedouins; see below.

show that the idea of continuous prophecy lingered for centuries, and, until modern times, even popped up among radical Shiites.[95]

Keeping the focus on early Islam, the sources give glimpses of several prophetic or messianic movements. Sometimes it is difficult to distinguish between the two, as most prophets were also ready to lead a movement against worldly and unjust government. They, in fact, were often forced to do so, as the Sunni system had no place for would-be prophets.[96] One source demonstrating the importance of would-be prophets in the first one and a half centuries of Islam is eschatological literature. Like their Jewish and Christian counterparts, Islamic apocalypses and eschatological texts are a valuable source for events suppressed or harmonized in later historical writings. The reconstruction of early Islam has in recent times relied much on this material.

The appearance of false prophets, as they are described in Islamic literature,[97] is one of the signs of the last days. In ad-Dānī's *as-Sunan al-wārida* 861–864, there are five *ḥadīth*s (nos. 441–445) mentioning false prophets, who seem to have been a cause of anxiety and thus a real threat to circles that invented and circulated *ḥadīth*s.[98] The point in these five *ḥadīth*s is similar. In all of them, the Prophet warns his nation about false prophets:

> (no. 441) The Last Hour will not come before nearly thirty lying dajjāls[99] will be sent, each one claiming to be the Messenger of God.

---

95 An interesting modern case is the eighteenth-century Shaykhīya movement, out of which the Bābīya grew in the nineteenth century; see, e.g., Henri Corbin, *En Iran islamien: Aspects spirituels et philosophiques* (vols. 1–4; Paris: Gallimard, 1971–1972), 4:205–300, and Smith, *Babi and Baha'i Religions.*

96 Many of these prophets who gained political importance—and were subsequently executed—are listed in Friedmann, "Finality," 194–96.

97 The Christian polemics against false prophets (already in Matt 7:15) may have been known to Muslim authors.

98 It might not be superfluous to recall that these "false prophets" were no threat to Islam: they provided a rival interpretation.

99 *Dajjāl,* from Syriac *daggālā* 'liar', usually refers to the false messiah, the Antichrist, but it is also used in the sense of "false prophet." In no. 445 (= Nuʿaym ibn Ḥammād, in *Kitāb al-Fitan* [1414; ed. Suhayl Zakkār; Beirut: Dār al-Fikr, 1993], 317), the number of *dajjāls* is raised to seventy-odd. Even the Antichrist first claims to be a prophet; see Ibn al-Munādī, *Malāḥim,* 249 (= Nuʿaym ibn Ḥammād, in *Fitan,* 326, and cf. 330).

(no. 442)[100] In my nation there will be thirty liars, each one of which claims to be a prophet, but I am the Seal of the Prophets. There will be no prophets after me.

Although these *ḥadīth*s offer no details, the general direction is clear. Many inspired religious aspirants saw themselves as new prophets, whose task was to maintain inspired, direct contact with God.

Iran, the formerly Zoroastrian state, seems to have been the most active hotbed of prophets, some of whom, like al-Muqannaʿ, "the Veiled Prophet of Khorasan" of the late eighth century,[101] probably had a Zoroastrian background. Others, like Bayān ibn Simʿān, who ascended to heaven, was anointed by God, and ordered to convey God's message to humankind,[102] undoubtedly found their inspiration in the biblical tradition. In a strict sense, these prophets did not continue Arabian prophecy, but belong to Christian, Jewish, or Zoroastrian paradigms. They were transplants from traditions other than Islamic. Nevertheless, their presence within the Islamic community is remarkable, and most of their followers seem to have called themselves "Muslims" and seen themselves within the Islamic tradition. A part of the population that may have been too ready to back new prophets were the bedouins; they are—together with women and Jews—often described among the followers of the Antichrist.[103]

In Ibn al-Munādī, *Malāḥim,* 259, Muḥammad is quoted as giving his verdict on Musaylima, who is among thirty false messiahs (*al-masīḥ ad-dajjāl*), referring in this case to false prophets. The *ḥadīth* is anachronistic—the eschatological speculation gained strength only several decades later[104]—and, consequently, it does not concern the historical Musaylima or the other *ridda* prophets, who had been vanquished

---

100 Also in, e.g., Ibn al-Munādī, *Malāḥim,* 113. Other versions of the *ḥadīth* are listed in Friedmann, "Finality," 196, n. 67.

101 *Tabari* 29:196–197. He was executed in 779 or soon after. See also Elton L. Daniel, *The Political and Social History of Khurasan under Abbasid Rule, 747–820* (Bibliotheca Islamica; Minneapolis and Chicago: Iran-America Foundation, 1979), 137–47.

102 E.g., [pseudo]-an-Nāshiʾ al-Akbar, *Uṣūl,* §60 (Josef van Ess, *Frühe muʿtazilitische Häresiographie: Zwei Werke des Nāšiʾ al-Akbar [gest. 293 H.]* [Beiruter Texte und Studien 11; Wiesbaden and Beirut: Franz Steiner, 1971], 9–70 [in Arabic]), translated in Hämeen-Anttila, "Descent."

103 E.g., Ibn al-Munādī, *Malāḥim,* 250–51, and often. See also Nuʿaym ibn Ḥammād, *Fitan,* 331.

104 The qurʾānic last day, and hence Muḥammad's view of eschatology, is a punishment which befalls the sinful people all of a sudden (*baghtatan;* Qur. 6:31 and often); there is no time for eschatological signs or persons.

years before this *ḥadīth* was fabricated. Rather, it is directed against later prophetic movements.[105] The classical Islamic authors mainly regarded these prophets as extremist (*ghulāt*) Shiites, a category without historical reality before the mid–eighth century. In fact, the early *ghulāt* movements should be seen as gnostic sects surfacing under the cover of the new religion. The moderate Shiite movement, which evolved as Twelver Shiism in the tenth century, accepted some *ghulāt* ideas, and the Shiite Imam shares many features with these early prophets. Divine messages were received by the Imam, and although the classical Shiite sources make a clear distinction between *waḥy* 'revelation', which only the prophets receive, and *ilhām* 'inspiration', which the Imams receive, there are traces of a more flexible terminology in the eighth century. At that time, the *Rūḥ* 'the Spirit' also brought revelations to the Imams, by which they were to guide their followers.[106]

Summary

In pre-Islamic times, the prophets were part of an Arabian tradition, with probably only faint influence from the biblical tradition. The pre-Islamic, inspired holy men were of two types. The first was the inspired soothsayer or *kāhin*, whose role was to answer questions for a price. These *kāhins* had no followers and no universal moral message, and their authority depended on societal acceptance, not on inherent authority. In contrast to diviners, the *kāhins* do not seem to have used accessorics, such as arrows, in their work. They received verbal inspiration from a supernatural power. The second group consisted of itinerant prophets, to whom Muḥammad originally belonged, and who conveyed a moral message from God to their audience. Hūd and Ṣāliḥ, the qur'ānically attested Arab prophets, should probably be counted in this class, as well as Musaylima and other *ridda* prophets. Neither the *kāhins* nor the itinerant prophets were organized, as far as sources allow, even though the sanctuaries on the peninsula would have made this possible.

---

105 Nuʿaym ibn Ḥammād, *Fitan*, 316, sets this event one month before the death of Muḥammad. Another version appears in ibid., 334–35.

106 See, in general, Mohammad Ali Amir-Moezzi, *The Divine Guide in Early Shiʿism: The Sources of Esotericism in Islam* (Albany: State University of New York Press, 1994).

During the career of Muḥammad, Arabian prophecy went through a biblicalization, and the indigenous tradition was molded to fit the biblical concept of prophecy as viewed by the Arabs. This biblical influence started during the Yathrib period of Muḥammad's life and continued posthumously, when his biography was molded to fit biblical models. The "pagan" Arabian tradition of prophecy was buried under a reconstituted form. In the classical Islamic period, the Sunnites developed a theory of the Seal of the Prophets, interpreted to mean that the final message of God to humankind had been delivered through Muḥammad and no further messages could be received; in a word, prophecy was limited to history and had no contemporary meaning. Shiite Islam followed less eagerly, and the Shiite Imam has always retained some prophetic features, although the term *waḥy* 'revelation' is avoided. The Imam, however, remains a direct channel to God and God's commands and fulfills many prophetic functions. In addition, there remained many marginal sects, later regarded as extremist Shiites, who received outside influences[107] and developed messianic and prophetic movements, which usually were involved with social disturbance. These movements are special cases of Islamic prophecy, but not direct descendants of Arabian prophecy.

Thus the advent of Islam sounded the death knell for Arabian prophecy, gradually adapting it to biblical models. Yet the birth of Islamic culture brought widespread literacy and thus helped to preserve information concerning Arabian prophecy, even if in a distorted and tendentious form. Without Islam, no information concerning this oral tradition would have been preserved, and Arabian prophecy would have disappeared without a trace—perhaps like other forms of Semitic prophecy, which may have disappeared without the existence of writing to preserve them.

---

107 It must be remembered that Sunni Islam received such foreign influences, too, but from different sources.

Index of Ancient Documents

All Hebrew Bible citations follow MT numbering.

SIRAH

Index of Modern Authors Cited

Contributors

Hans M. Barstad teaches in the Faculty of Theology at the University of Oslo.

Lester L. Grabbe teaches in the Department of Theology at the University of Hull, England.

Jaakko Hämeen-Anttila teaches in the Department of Asian and African Studies at the University of Helsinki.

Herbert B. Huffmon teaches at Drew University in Madison, New Jersey.

Martti Nissinen teaches in the Department of Biblical Studies at the University of Helsinki.

David L. Petersen teaches at the Iliff School of Theology in Denver.

Karel van der Toorn teaches in the Faculty of Humanities at the University of Amsterdam.